Truth and Subjectivity, Faith and History

# Truth and Subjectivity, Faith and History

### Kierkegaard's Insights for Christian Faith

VARUGHESE JOHN

◐PICKWICK *Publications* • Eugene, Oregon

TRUTH AND SUBJECTIVITY, FAITH AND HISTORY
Kierkegaard's Insights for Christian Faith

Copyright © 2012 Varughese John. All rights reserved. Except for brief quotations in critical publications or reviews, no part of this book may be reproduced in any manner without prior written permission from the publisher. Write: Permissions, Wipf and Stock Publishers, 199 W. 8th Ave., Suite 3, Eugene, OR 97401.

Pickwick Publications
An Imprint of Wipf and Stock Publishers
199 W. 8th Ave., Suite 3
Eugene, OR 97401

www.wipfandstock.com

ISBN 13: 978-1-61097-894-1

*Cataloging-in-Publication data:*

John, Varughese.

Truth and subjectivity, faith and history : Kierkegaard's insights for Christian faith / Varughese John.

xviii + 160 p. ; 23 cm. Includes bibliographical references and index.

ISBN 13: 978-1-61097-894-1

1. Kierkegaard, Søren, 1813–1855—Religion. 2. Truth. 3. Christianity—Philosophy. I. Title.

B4378 J56 2012

Manufactured in the U.S.A.

To
My parents,
A.V. John and Susamma John

# Contents

*Foreword ix*
*Preface xiii*
*Abbreviations xv*

**PART I** **Truth and Subjectivity**
1. On the Very Idea of Truth 3
2. Truthing through Subjectivity 34
3. Being in the Truth: Re-engaging Climacus' Devout Idolater 59

**PART II** **History and Faith**
4. Understanding Historical Religious Knowledge for Faith 73
5. Historical Research and its Sufficiency for Faith 98
6. Kierkegaardian Insights for Christian Apologetics 123

*Bibliography 147*
*Index 155*

# Foreword

ANALYZING THE CONCEPT OF truth is a challenging task. Philosophical concepts of truth turn up in so many forms that it sometimes seems as if there are as many concepts of truth as there are philosophers.

In fact, sometimes the word "truth" itself appears to mean the opposite for one thinker as it does for another. For example, the father of modern European philosophy, René Descartes, takes for granted just those truths that the father of existentialism, Søren Kierkegaard, questions most severely; whereas Kierkegaard assumes much that Descartes subjects to radical doubt.[1] In this respect the two men are like mirror images of each other. Thus in his *Discourse on Method* Descartes proposes to go along, in his personal life, with contemporary social mores and conventional religiosity but at the same time to question, methodologically, the existence of the external world and even of his own self; while Kierkegaard accepts without question the existence of the external world, devotes much of his writing to urging readers to develop their own selves, and concludes his life with a relentless attack upon the social and religious establishment of nineteenth-century Denmark. In these respects, what the one accepts, the other attacks, and vice versa.

Still, are the two men really that far apart in their understandings of the nature of truth? Or are they not rather merely following different but complementary paths, when Descartes insists upon mathematical certainty as the basis for experimental science, and Kierkegaard stresses the importance of religious uncertainty within the life of personal faith?

In some respects Descartes and Kierkegaard are very close indeed. Granted, the two disagree fundamentally regarding the basis of mathematical certainty, since, like most philosophers and mathematicians today, Kierkegaard distinguishes more sharply than Descartes between

---

1. David Swenson, *Something About Kierkegaard* (Minneapolis: Augsburg, 1945), 111.

mathematics and experimental science.² Such disagreement, however, should not be allowed to overshadow the respect for experimental science that Kierkegaard, along with others of his time, shares with Descartes. Like seventeenth-century France, early nineteenth-century Denmark was experiencing an explosion of scientific discoveries, of which Kierkegaard was well aware. Kierkegaard was, for example, personally acquainted with Hans Christian Ørsted (1777–1851), the great Copenhagen physicist and chemist after whom the unit of magnetic field strength is named, and he maintained a life-long friendship with his brother-in-law Peter William Lund, a distinguished paleontologist who identified many new species while doing research in the jungles of Brazil.

Where Kierkegaard differs most obviously from Descartes is in the way he distinguishes both mathematical and scientific truths from another, more personal, kind of truth. In one of his early upbuilding discourses, for example, he contrasts "indifferent" truths, such as the truths of mathematics and science, which hold whether or not a person accepts them, and "concerned" truths, regarding which it makes a decisive difference to an individual whether or not they are "truths for him."³ What Kierkegaard says about such "concerned" truths shows that he is thinking about the goals or principles an individual adopts, explicitly or implicitly, to guide one's whole life—the truths, as he once put it in an early journal entry, for which a person might be "willing to live and die."⁴ Of course, such truths make no claim to universal validity, but without adopting any such truths a person may simply drift through life without direction.

Nonetheless, there is no reason to think that Descartes also cannot accommodate this Kierkegaardian distinction between two kinds of truths, since Descartes himself freely admits that he had struggled through his personal decisions; and, besides, it is hard to imagine any rational person insisting upon mathematical certainty before making personal decisions at the crucial junctures in one's own life. At any rate, Kierkegaard's pseudonym Johannes de Silentio presents that picture of Descartes' life. Descartes, he writes, "did not shout 'Fire! Fire!' and make it obligatory for everyone to doubt, for Descartes was a quiet and solitary thinker, not a shouting night

---

2. JP, 1: 197.
3. "Think About Your Creator . . . ," EUD, 233–34.
4. JP, 5: 5100.

watchman; he modestly let it be known that his method had significance only for him and was partly the result of his earlier warped knowledge."[5]

Whatever the case may have been with Descartes, however, such philosophical modesty does not characterize the rationalist period that follows in Europe, and by the early to middle nineteenth century it has gone entirely out of fashion. Instead, many of the popular thinkers of the nineteenth century draw a distinction between "objective" (or "rational") truths, on the one hand, and "subjective" truths, on the other; and what Kierkegaard calls "concerned" truths they are apt to see as "subjective" and thereby, at best, second-rate, if they do not consign them to the scrap heap of irrationality altogether.

Kierkegaard's response to his contemporaries' classification of "concerned truths" as "subjective" is creative but also, one must admit, wide open to misunderstanding: he has his best-known philosophical pseudonym, Johannes Climacus, defend the thesis that "subjectivity is truth." Thus, even though readers are warned over and over again that Climacus is a "humorist" and that he is conducting his argument with elaborate irony and indirection, it is not surprising that some careless readers mistake what Climacus is doing and think that he is supporting the truth, not merely of "concerned" truths but of subjective claims of any kind.

A big part of the challenge Varughese John takes on in the present volume, therefore, is to sort out the various aspects of this confusion over subjective truth. Since that task is formidable, his analysis has had to range widely, involving topics such as dogmatism and relativism, modernism and postmodernism, scientific and historical truths, and the like, all of which are interconnected; but to my mind he carries off the investigation very well. What fascinates me especially about Professor John's approach, moreover, is the way he draws upon key aspects of the classical and contemporary traditions of India. Up to now the names of figures such as Rāmānujā and Amartya Sen, for example, have appeared all too rarely on the pages of discussions of Kierkegaard's works, but, with this study as a model, one may hope that they will appear more and more frequently in the future.

*Andrew J. Burgess, Professor of Philosophy Emeritus,*
*The University of New Mexico*

---

5. FT, 6.

# Preface

TRUTH AND SUBJECTIVITY, FAITH *and History* is the result of a personal journey that was embarked upon ever since I first encountered Kierkegaard during my seminary days. His writings characteristically imposed themselves upon me as a reader, by entering the innermost depths of my thinking and conscience. His exceptional ability to rudely shake someone under an illusion of being in truth as a Christian into despair, by making Christianity more difficult than imagined, just seems to have worked in my case. However, to the one who despairs about not being the Christian one ought to be—a feeling that Kierkegaard himself struggled with—he is quick to clarify, as he does in *The Point of View*: "Christianity is just as gentle as it is rigorous, just as gentle, that is, infinitely gentle. When the infinite requirement is heard and affirmed, is heard and affirmed in all its infinitude, then grace is offered, or grace offers itself, to which the single individual, each one individually, can then have recourse as I do; and then it works out all right." This tension between the rigor and gentleness of Christianity imposes upon one the misery of rigor and the joy of grace, an imposition which characterized his own personal and spiritual journey, one that he has successfully passed on to at least some of his readers, including me.

My journey has been truly enriched by far more than those people listed here, yet some deserve a special mention. My stays at the Howard V. Hong and Edna H. Hong Kierkegaard Library at St. Olaf College, Northfield, MN, both as a Summer Research Scholar and as a Kierkegaard House Foundation Fellow, were greatly rewarding. Much of this book was put together during my stay at the Library as a Kierkegaard House Foundation Fellow.

A special thanks to the Kierkegaard House Foundation and the Friends of Kierkegaard for their generous support. I express my deepest gratitude to Gordon D. Marino, the Curator, and Cynthia Wales Lund, the Assistant Curator, of the Kierkegaard Library. Their warmth and support

## Preface

continue to transform the Library from a dry research establishment, to a lively, interactive, and friendly place. You are truly wonderful people!

I thank Erik Hong, the Olsons, and Ameeta and Craig Rice, who went the extra mile to make our stay at 3, Lincoln Ln, Northfield, the most memorable time in the United States. I specially thank members of the Immanuel Bible Chapel, Hastings, who welcomed us into their church and homes, turning our hard Minnesota winter into a pleasant one.

I thank my editor Robin Parry for his excellent and skillful support. I thank Andrew Burgess for writing the *Foreword* and for the great support he is for Kierkegaard research in India. I thank my good friends Myron B. Penner, Peder Jothan, Richard Nelson, and Gabriel Merigala, who graciously read through my manuscript and gave useful comments. The flaws that remain are entirely mine and not theirs. I thank Elcy Padmanabhan, Selena George, Prashanti Mikayla, and Mary Varughese for their excellent editorial help with the manuscript.

I thank my family—my parents, all my in-laws, my sisters and their families—who constantly prayed and supported me in every way. Finally, I thank my greatest supporters—my wife, Mary and our children, Ashish, and Preetha—who bore the brunt of cancelled vacations and deprived family time, gracefully.

I thank the editors of the following journals for the permissions granted to republish some sections of this book which appeared in their journals.

- "'Truth' in an Ethnocentric Relativistic Scheme: A Critique" of Chapter 1 appeared as "Truth in Postmodernity: Reengaging Rorty and Kierkegaard." *Dharma Deepika* 22 (2005) 51–62.

- Chapter 3 appeared as "Being in the Truth: Climacus' Devout Idolater from within Rāmānuja's *Viśiṣṭādvaitic* Tradition." *Acta Kierkegaardiana* 5 (2011) 78–88.

- Parts of Chapter 4 and 6 appeared as "Historical Christian Beliefs and Apologetics in a Hindu Context." *Dharma Deepika* 26 (2007) 42–49.

- Section B of Chapter 6 appeared as "A Sense of History and Apologetics in a Hindu Context." *Missiology: An International Review* 36 (2008) 219–26.

All Bible quotations are from the Revised Standard Version.

# Abbreviations

WORKS PUBLISHED BY KIERKEGAARD, unless otherwise indicated, are cited from *Kierkegaard Works*, translated and edited by Howard V. Hong and Edna H. Hong, Princeton University Press from 1978 to 2000.

| | |
|---|---|
| BA | *The Book on Adler*. vol. 24, 1995. |
| CUP | *Concluding Unscientific Postscript*. (2 vols.) vol. 12, 1992. |
| EO | *Either/Or*. (2 vols.) vols. 3 and 4, 1987. |
| EUD | *Eighteen Upbuilding Discourses*. vol. 5, 1990. |
| FSE | *For Self-Examination*. vol. 21, 1990. |
| FT | *Fear and Trembling / Repetition*. vol. 6, 1983. |
| JP | *Søren Kierkegaard's Journals and Papers*, edited and translated by Howard V. Hong and Edna H. Hong, assisted by Gregor Melantschuk, 7 vols. Bloomington IN: Indiana University Press, 1967–79. (Cited according to entry number.) |
| PC | *Practice in Christianity*. vol. 20, 1991. |
| PF | *Philosophical Fragments*. vol. 7, 1985. |
| PV | *Point of View*. vol. 22, 1998. |
| SUD | *The Sickness Unto Death*. vol. 19, 1980. |
| SUD | *The Sickness Unto Death*. Translated by Alastair Hannay. London: Penguin, 1989. |
| TA | *Two Ages*. vol. 14, 1978. |
| UDVS | *Upbuilding Discourses in Various Spirits*. vol. 15, 1993. |
| WA | *Without Authority*. vol. 18, 1997. |
| WL | *Works of Love*. vol. 16, 1995. |

# Introduction

CHRISTIANITY HAS DISTINGUISHED ITSELF from other beliefs and philosophies by its claim to truth. Corresponding to the contours of the truth discourses of the past decades, Christian appropriations of truth primarily assumed a propositional frame. While it would be erroneous to discount the value of propositional truth, such a preoccupation resulted in reducing Christian faith primarily to holding propositionally accurate beliefs. Kierkegaard writes in *The Point of View*, "Christianity still exists and in its truth, but as a *teaching*, as *doctrine*. What has been abolished and forgotten (and this can be said without exaggeration), however, is being a Christian, what it means to be a Christian; or what has been lost, what seems to exist no longer, is the ideal picture of being a Christian."[6] It is upon those who presupposed the truth of Christian beliefs, and yet were "under an illusion when they call themselves Christians,"[7] that Kierkegaard sought to impose the authentic dimension of truth, as subjectivity.

Kierkegaard's emphasis on *Truth as Subjectivity* is discussed in the first section (chapters 1–3) of the book. In Chapter 1, after introducing the modern and postmodern approaches to truth, Rorty's abandonment of objectivity in favor of communal solidarity as a ground for truth, is critiqued. The limits of a logico-semantic truth discourse, and the legitimacy of the postmodern suspicion of truth-claims, supports the entry of Kierkegaard as a helpful conversation partner to address the modern and postmodern deviations. Kierkegaard contrasts Christ (who reveals truth from without) with Socrates (who locates truth within the individual), thus distinguishing Christianity from every other philosophy and privileging Christian revelation over human reason. Chapter 2 examines the centrality of the concept of human self to the question of a truth-pursuit. As the human self is in the process of becoming, it conceives that the highest truth is attained by

6. PV, 129–30.
7. PV, 42.

## Introduction

relating to God, who establishes the self. Following this, Chapter 3 examines one of the most popular parables of Kierkegaard (that of the penitent idolater), to understand more practically what Kierkegaard means by subjectivity. Does he mean just "sincerity" or does subjectivity involve something more? The parable is illustrated by locating the idolater within a popular Indian philosophical school called *Viśiṣṭādvaita*. It argues that there cannot be a proper understanding of subjectivity outside Christ and His revelation.

The second section, *Faith and History* (chapters 4–6), examines the value of historical research for Christian faith. Addressing the question of miracles, and the rationalist and empiricist conceptions of history, Chapter 4 lays out the effect popular views of history have had on Christian faith, leading some to separate the Jesus of history from the Christ of faith, and some to use positivist calculus to prove the truth of Christian beliefs. Chapter 5 addresses the importance of history for Christian faith, while emphasizing that historical inquiry cannot be the basis for it. It also discusses Kierkegaard's understanding of a believer as contemporaneous with Christ, in response to Lessing's problem of the "ugly broad ditch." Following an examination of the role of evidence for faith, Chapter 6 explores ways in which Kierkegaardian insights could inform Christian apologetics. Apart from looking at the epistemic status of faith, it also discusses Kierkegaard's Pneumatology. It also explores Kierkegaardian insights for apologetics in the South Asian context, with its unique sense of history.

# PART I

## Truth and Subjectivity

# 1

## On the Very Idea of Truth

*The difficulty is not to understand what Christianity is but to become and to be a Christian. — CUP 1:560*

"What is truth?" asked Pilate, without expecting an answer. Over the centuries, philosophers have found it difficult to answer this question conclusively. Is truth a substance or a quality, a body of knowledge or the character of a statement? Where truth is understood as the property of a statement, it assumes a representational character as the right representation of reality, since a great number of statements—thought, spoken, or written—are about reality. Consequently, truth takes the shape of the varied understandings of reality entertained by philosophers and lay people. The most common notion of viewing the world is the "realist view," which sees reality as something "out there," independent of our minds. A realist notion is also dependent on the correspondence theory of truth, which sees truth representationally as that which corresponds to facts. Its origins go back to Aristotle. He wrote in his *Metaphysics*, "To say of what is that it is not, or of what is not that it is, is false, while to say of what is that it is, and of what is not that it is not, is true" (1011b). However, all along there have been skeptics who have challenged the possibility of definite truth. There are competing understandings to the realists' position in anti-realism, idealism, conceptualism, relativism, etc., each of which has different strokes and shades of expression.

The difficulty in defining truth is that all the traditional theories of truth such as the correspondence, coherence, and pragmatic theories merely presuppose truth and do not really define it. Since truth in general evades conclusive decisiveness, knowing and possessing it become equally evasive. Yet, underneath the vagaries surrounding differing understandings of truth, one can notice human nature in its unending pursuit of truth. Irrespective of one's nationality, religion, or vocation, the pursuit of truth has always been regarded as an important part of human life. Whether it is the pain of a life-threatening crisis that sets one off on such a pursuit or merely being weary of pleasure, human nature is designed to seek truth. The question of truth, therefore, seems to be essentially connected to the very essence of humankind.

This issue will engage our discussion in the first section of the book. Following a brief background on the modern and postmodern understandings of truth, Kierkegaard will be brought into the conversation. While most modern and contemporary discussions treat a pursuit of truth as primarily a cognitive "knowing" of what it is, Kierkegaard focuses not only on the "what" but also emphasizes "how" truth ought to affect our being, or the self. Thus having Kierkegaard as the conversation partner in our truth discourse is to accentuate the essential connection between truth and being. This oft-ignored Kierkegaardian emphasis offers a richer understanding of truth. To understand Kierkegaard's objection to an "objective" pursuit of truth, I shall clarify what it means to raise the question of truth in an objective sense. Raising the question of truth in an objective sense is not the same as understanding reality as objectively real. It is perfectly plausible to raise the question of truth objectively and yet not see the world as objectively real. Kierkegaard's objection, therefore, should not be understood as a denial of objective truth but as a concern for what is amiss in raising the question of truth purely objectively.

## The Idea of Truth in Modernity and Postmodernity

### Modernity and the Idea of Truth

The early seventeenth-century philosopher, René Descartes (1596–1650), who is referred to as the "father of modern philosophy," considered truth to be a finished product. Truth was conceived as something that could be conclusively understood with our rational thinking. Thus, the Enlightenment approach was marked by an optimism that truth was out there, and could be discovered and mastered. The notion of truth was intricately tied to the emancipation of the individual—emancipation via Enlightenment/reason and the practice of democratic ideals, or through a socialistic commitment and revolution that liberated the individual from the clutches of the aristocracy.

The modern-Enlightenment thinking pursued truth in a narrow sense, accentuating merely the rational aspect of truth, where an objective pursuit became the most important mechanism to unearth the reality that was out there. The naturalistic assumptions that were gaining predominance undermined the metaphysical and theological dimensions of truth by reducing reality essentially to the empirically verifiable material world. This reduction was a convenient one in that truth-pursuits did not have to deal with the vagaries of the metaphysical dimensions of life. This entailed not only that truth could be arrived at through reason but also that the self assumed the position of an impersonal observer, who sees the world *sub specie aeterni* (a Latin expression to denote a "perspective of the eternal" or God's-eye-view), devoid of an existential identity.

The term "objective truth" came to refer to reality that could be verified by the rules laid out by the logical positivists of the early twentieth century.[1] Logical positivists employed empiricism and rationalism to make observational evidence a condition for knowledge and rendered metaphysical, ethical, and theological statements meaningless. Although those committed to logical positivism were a small group of philosophers within Western academia, the impact of its naturalistic thinking, in the aftermath of Enlightenment, was nonetheless powerful and garnered tremendous influence. Yet, a majority of humanity within non-Western cultures, mostly untouched by modernity, held onto some form of religious belief and never reduced reality or their understanding of truth to merely the natural world. "Reality" and "truth" for them included a world beyond the material and a belief in the supernatural. Furthermore, since religious beliefs in general viewed the supernatural as superior to the natural, it relegated a higher status for the spiritual over the material.

However, the religious conception of truth followed its own course, often by morphing itself in accordance to the contemporary theories of truth. Both modern and postmodern understandings of truth tend to swerve away from the Christian perspective of associating truth with the

---

1. Ayer, *Language Truth and Logic*, 13–29.

being of God. Perhaps the real disservice to the Christian conception of truth has come from within the church's deliberate subversions of the truth, typified in the papal invention of several "religious truths" when the papal treasuries began to dry up. Perhaps Emperor Constantine's "conversion" experience itself is suspect, as an effort to appease the sizeable and growing Christian population in his empire. Hence, his vision of the cross with the phrase, which is more popular in its Latin rendition, *in hoc signo vinces* (meaning "by this sign, be victorious") that he saw during one of his expeditions, could be seen as being politically motivated rather than as spiritual obedience to a divine command. Likewise, medieval European history tells stories of the political heads of the church-state abrogating personal freedoms and individual rights. Such an instrumentalist view of truth, whether in the secular world or within the church, has persistently sought to manipulate reality to harness it for personal gains in the garb of progress.

## Postmodernity and the Idea of Truth

Contrary to expectations, the early twentieth century saw a destruction of human life and optimism to an extent never witnessed before. The World Wars, gas chambers, and atomic bombs could hardly be counted as progress. The ensuing disillusionment with the Enlightenment project replaced modernistic optimism with pessimism and nihilism in postmodernity. The chasm between human expectation of progress and the reality of the devastation of structures and of hope resulted in an era of suspicion. Thus, in postmodernism, facts are seen not as truths but as interpretations, accompanied by a rampant suspicion of truth-claims, because reality is fundamentally viewed as invented and nothing more. In the words of Friedrich Nietzsche (1844–1900), considered a vanguard of postmodernism, "Truths are illusions we have forgotten are illusions." He says, "Truth is a mobile army of metaphors, metonyms and anthropomorphisms."[2] Even logic and morality are subject to flux. "Truth is not fixed but shifting. It can be mobilized and deployed according to the interests and purposes of its claimants who turn out to be manipulators. Truth is entirely mutable and offers no foundation at all."[3]

Nietzsche's truest follower, Michel Foucault (1926–1984), further illustrates the postmodern suspicion of truth. The application of reason in

---

2. Nietzsche, "On Truth and Lie," 46.
3. Bridger, "Counseling in a Postmodern Context," 282.

truth-pursuit in a knowledge-based society is seen as no different from the political power pursuits of the medieval times. In the Enlightenment project, knowledge became a new instrument of power. Both politics and knowledge legitimized power. Thus reflecting on modern society, Foucault argues, "It is necessary to think of the political problems of intellectuals not in terms of 'science' and 'ideology,' but in terms of 'truth' and 'power.'"[4] "Truth," Foucault suggests, "is linked in a circular relation with systems of power which produce and sustain it, and to effects of power which it induces and which extends it. A 'regime' of truth."[5] The Nietzsche-Foucaultian power connection with truth-claims is visible in the modern Enlightenment context where reason parades itself as the new power apparatus. In short, the postmodern analysis tends to relativize the idea of truth and reality due to the impossibility of a value-free, neutral knowledge. Knowledge is, therefore, perspectival in nature and calls for a multiplicity of viewpoints to interpret a heterogeneous reality. Thus, since there are no fixed meanings that correspond to fixed reality, one cannot arrive at definitive truth.

Jean-François Lyotard (1924–98) likewise analyzes the legitimizing of metanarratives by philosophy as the center of modernity. As Westphal recounts, Lyotard analyzes two such overarching metanarratives: that of Hegel and of Marx. Hegel presented the "story of speculative narrative," which sought to legitimize "modern, Western humanity as the absolute subject whose knowledge of itself as such is absolute knowing."[6] Marx, on the other hand, presented the "emancipation narrative," which sought "to legitimize the proletarian revolution that will abolish private property and usher in the classless society."[7] It is in the need for a rejection of such overarching views of Enlightenment thinking that Lyotard defines postmodernism as "incredulity towards metanarratives."[8] In postmodernity, the general thinking embodies the statement, "the truth is that there are no Truths."

---

4. Rabinow, *The Foucault Reader*, 74.
5. Ibid., 74
6. Westphal, *Overcoming Onto-theology*, xiv.
7. Ibid., xiv.
8. Lyotard, *The Postmodern Condition*, xxiv.

# Truth and Subjectivity, Faith and History

## "Truth" in an Ethnocentric Relativistic Scheme: A Critique

While some are entirely dismissive of truth-claims, Richard McKay Rorty[9] (1931–2007), one of the most influential postmodern pragmatists, argues that "truth" is created and located purely within the sociocultural context. For Rorty, "truth" is essentially established within sociocultural or ethnic communities, which become the agents that establish the validity of truth and reality. Thus, we are to be led by what works by solidarity and not by any a priori idea of objectivity. He says, "The question whether truth and rationality has an intrinsic nature, whether we ought to have a positive theory about either topic, is just the question of whether our self-description ought to be constructed around a relation to human nature or around a relation to a particular collection of human beings, whether we should desire objectivity or solidarity."[10]

Thus, the Rortian claim is that truth is not trans-cultural and universal but created and furthered by solidarity within communities. By locating truth purely within the human discursive enterprise, Rorty holds to a type of ethnocentric relativism that dismisses any transcendental bearing upon the understanding of truth. A relativist notion of truth denies truth in the realist sense that sees reality as objective and as existing independent of our minds. Pradhan argues that Rortian ethnocentric relativism leads to two dogmas. "One is that truth is relative to a conceptual scheme and the other is that truth is a product of human interests. The former can be called the dogma of conceptual relativization and the latter the dogma of ethnocentrism."[11]

On the periphery, ethnocentric relativism is not total relativism—a claim that anything goes. Rather, it is a claim that the validity, or standard of truth, is established within a given cultural context. That is, the truth of an issue is relative to the conceptual framework of the ethnic society, where the dynamics of a community are the deciding factors in its own interest. According to Rorty, "For the pragmatist . . . 'knowledge' is, like 'truth,' simply a compliment paid to the beliefs which we think so well justified that, for the moment, further justification is not needed. An inquiry into the nature of knowledge can, on this view, only be a socio-historical account

---

9. Incidentally, Rorty's maternal grandfather, Walter Rauschenbusch, was a central figure in the Social Gospel movement of the early twentieth century.
10. Rorty, *Objectivity Relativism and Truth*, 24.
11. Pradhan, "On the Very Idea of Relative Truth," 46.

of how various people have tried to reach agreement on what to believe."[12] Accordingly, truth is the result of a common agreement within a given community, on the basis of some stabilizing factors that work for the good of that community. Thus, objectivity is replaced by solidarity or shared aims of the community. Rorty's pragmatism goes well with his ethnocentric relativism as truth is decided on the basis of its practical utility and the workability of a belief or idea within a community. For postmodernists like Rorty and Foucault, inquiry into knowledge and truth is an inquiry into how these concepts have traditionally worked or have been used. It is not an inquiry into the essence of truth or knowledge.

Rortian ethnocentric sentiment rejects the supposedly "neutral" evaluative language of an alien cultural vocabulary. In his typical rejection of the realist position, Rorty says, "It is useless to ask whether one vocabulary rather than another is closer to reality. For different vocabularies serve different purposes, and there is no such thing as a purpose that is closer to reality than another purpose. . . . Nothing is conveyed in saying . . . that the vocabulary in which we predict the motion of a planet is more in touch with how things really are than the vocabulary in which we assign the planet an astrological influence."[13] Central to the rejection of any trans-cultural reasoning is the presupposition that cultures are discontinuous. At the very least, there is a committed downplaying of cross-cultural continuity based on a moral or logico-rational discourse. The relativist builds on the availability of multiple conceptual schemes.[14] There is also a separation of the conceptual scheme and the experiential content. Accordingly, truth is not something absolute but is our conceptual construction and since multiple conceptual schemes are possible, the relativists argue, there is no single impression of truth that pervades all possible conceptual schemes. Thus, the relativist concludes that for each conceptual scheme (for example, $C_1$, $C_2$, $C_3$, and so on), there is a corresponding truth ($T_1$, $T_2$, $T_3$, and so on). As Newton-Smith puts it, "The central relativist idea is that what is true for one tribe, social group or age might not be true for another tribe, social group or age."[15] Accordingly, for a relativist, that which is considered true or real holds only within a given conceptual scheme.

---

12. Rorty, *Objectivity, Relativism and Truth*, 24.
13. See "Introduction," in John P. Murphy's *Pragmatism*, 3.
14. See Davidson, "On the Very Idea of a Conceptual Scheme," 183–98.
15. Newton-Smith, "Relativism and the Possibility of Interpretation," 107.

## Truth and Subjectivity, Faith and History

Now the question is whether the availability of alternative conceptual schemes results in an unavoidable relativism or not. Does the multiplicity of conceptual schemes also mean the multiplicity of truth? The relativist argument is that if there are alternative conceptual schemes to construct and organize our experience, then alternative models of truth should also be possible. Ernest Gellner summarizes the relativist's predicament. He says, "The problem of relativism is whether there is one and only one world, in the end; whether all the divergent visions of reality can in the end be shown ... to be diverse aspects of one and the same objective world, whose diversity can itself be explained in terms of the properties or laws of that world."[16] In relativism, the realist view of the world is rejected and the existence of a single world behind all possible world-descriptions is denied, as there are as many worlds as there are world-descriptions or conceptual schemes. The assumption is that each world-description projects and invents its own world. To borrow an illustration: a mountain could present itself differently to a climber, a geologist, a painter, and so on, whose world-projections need not be interdependent. As a result, when there are competing conceptual schemes, they all could claim validity at the same time. Relativism in its strongest form—say total relativism—is committed to the view that alternative conceptual schemes inevitably lead to the existence of alternative worlds that are isolated from each other and have nothing in common.

Truth construed as relative leads to contradiction, for if every truth-claim is equally valid, what then could be the basis for preferring one truth-claim to another. As every truth-claim is disengaged from an endorsement of a reason that is not bound within the confines of the ethnic group, the validity of relativism itself is relative. A relativist position is inconsistent as the relativist truth-claim is either self-defeating or reintroduces absolutism through the back door. As Putnam argues, "That relativism is inconsistent is a truism among philosophers. After all, is it not obviously contradictory to hold a point of view while at the same time holding that no point of view is more justified or right than any other? ... If any point of view is as good as any other, then why isn't the point of view that relativism is false as good as any other?"[17]

In Rortian ethnocentric relativism, primacy is given to the community or ethnic group to arbiter the form and content of truth. It is to say that truth is what is made of it within the ethnic group. In effect, ethnocentric

16. Gellner, "Relativism and Universals," 186.
17. Putnam, *Reason, Truth and History*, 119.

relativism is qualitatively no different from total relativism. As P. K. Moser points out, the problem with ethnocentric relativism is "its appeal to *our* society as providing the only relevant procedures of justification for an intelligible characterization of the notion of justification. What reason have we to give our society such primacy—such a monopoly—by way of conceptual significance?"[18]

A further oversight of such a view becomes obvious when it presupposes that it is impossible to stand outside a given language or conceptual scheme. It is pivotal to note that the whole philosophical meta-discourse, including that of Rorty's ethnocentric relativism with all its prescriptive nuances, presumes to be applicable to more than a single culture. Or should we understand that Rorty confines the scope of his writings to the Anglo-Saxon world? I doubt he does. Does not Rorty then, in a sense, stand "outside" his own cultural milieu when he prescribes his ethnocentric relativism? In other words, Rorty overlooks the fact that our philosophical discourses occur at a *meta*-level—not discoursing merely within a culture, but about cultures themselves. If that is the case, as in a necklace, there seems to be a common rational thread, accessible to all cultures, stringing the beads of their particular conceptual schemes together.

Putnam argues, "Relativism, just as much as Realism, assumes that one can stand within one's language and outside it at the same time. In the case of Realism this is not an immediate contradiction, since the whole content of Realism lies in the claim that it makes sense to think of a God's-Eye View (or, better, of a "View from Nowhere"); but in the case of Relativism it constitutes a self-refutation."[19] The relativist position, which equally validates contesting viewpoints, cannot, at the same time and for that very reason, prefer a particular viewpoint. The relativist notion of truth also tends to confuse the distinction between truth and justification. Following Putnam's argument, Pradhan writes, "truth ceases to be a matter of justification *per se*, but of ideal and convergent justification which presupposes the notion of truth itself. Truth cannot be reduced to justification since justification can be defeated, but truth remains stable and intact."[20] It is also important to distinguish between the logical reasoning that is universal and one that is contextual. There are laws of thought, logical and mathematical, which,

---

18. Moser, *Philosophy after Objectivity*, 166–67.

19. Putnam, *Realism with a Human Face*, 23.

20. Pradhan, "On the Very Idea of Relative Truth," 54. Cf. Putnam, *Reason, Truth and History*, 54.

irrespective of ethnic traditions, are universal and there are also reasoning modes that are unique to particular traditions. While there was an overemphasis of the former at the expense of the latter in modern thinking, the postmodern reversal celebrates the particular traditional reasoning at the expense of the possibility of common reasoning. It is the very belief in a common reason that enables the possibility of evaluating the validity of different truth-claims, both intra-culturally and inter-culturally. In the words of Pradhan, "truth like reason goes beyond space and time while all the while being involved in time and history. In that sense truth is transcendent as well as immanent in that it is not a product of a temporal process though it applies to the temporal history of judgment-formation."[21]

The problem with a relativist notion of truth is that it functions today, not so much based on a logical argument but on its political correctness. While an objective philosophical definition of truth is impossible, a relativist notion of truth is a forthright contradiction. On the one hand, it is disastrous to put away reason from truth-discourses; and yet, truth evades a rationalistic, logico-semantic reduction.

## Pre-Theoretical Commitment

The postmodern discourses on truth have clarified that human beliefs about the world, life, its purpose, meaning, etc., are not necessarily conclusions arrived at the end of a deliberation. Some are merely pre-theoretical commitments and some are resolutions. In *Philosophical Fragments*, echoing Plato, Climacus[22] writes on the question of the existence of God: "If, namely, the god does not exist, then of course it is impossible to demonstrate it. But if he does exist, then it is foolishness to want to demonstrate it, since I, in the very moment the demonstration commences, would presuppose it not as doubtful—which a presupposition cannot be, inasmuch as it is a presupposition—but as decided, because otherwise I would not begin, easily perceiving that the whole thing would be impossible if he did not exist."[23] Climacus' argument, in a way, points to a person who approaches the facts of history from a pre-theoretical commitment and therefore proves nothing. Accordingly, in as much as the truth of a demonstration is already presupposed,

21. Pradhan, "On the Very Idea of Relative Truth," 54.

22. Although an unbeliever, Johannes Climacus, Kierkegaard's philosophical pseudonym, is not only aware of the Christian doctrines but also considers them true.

23. PF, 39.

nothing is proven. Climacus alerts us to the pre-theoretical beliefs that we tend to carry out our demonstration from rather than toward it. Like a lens, one's pre-theoretical commitments are not seen, but seen through. Not surprisingly, non-cognizance of one's pre-theoretical commitments makes one imagine that one's beliefs are indeed a result of inquiry and proof, rather than what they really are—pre-theoretical commitments.

A case in point for such non-cognizance was the Logical Positivists' attempt to undermine metaphysics, in their proposal of the "Verifiability Principle" as the criterion for establishing the meaningfulness of a statement.[24] According to the verifiability principle, a statement is meaningful only if it has perception terms as its predicate. The principle can be put forth as a simple proposition: "meaningful statements must have perception terms as its predicates." David Hugh Freeman points to an important problem by asking whether this statement is scientific or metaphysical. If scientific, then it would have had to have perception terms as its predicate; if metaphysical, then it happens to be the very thing it sought to undermine. Thus, Freeman concludes that, "the statement 'a meaningful statement is a statement which has a perception term as its predicate' is vague"[25] by its own criterion. As it is obvious, the Logical Positivists' criterion of meaning is not neutral as it remains a case of arguing from a conclusion rather than working towards a conclusion. It is therefore rightly asked whether this criterion of meaning is neutral. Besides the incongruity of any belief that does not bring itself under the criterion it sets up, the Logical Positivists' stance reveals that there are beliefs that are argued from and are not established by a process of sound reasoning. Yet, unlike the Positivists' criterion, there would be a legitimate way of holding beliefs that are not inferred, as in the case of "basic beliefs" in Alvin Plantinga's sense of the term.

By basic beliefs, Plantinga means those beliefs that are held not on the basis of other beliefs.[26] They are beliefs that are not inferred or arrived at; rather, they are beliefs that are argued from, held without any evidential support from some other beliefs. While a basic belief is not based on any other belief, it could provide the basis for other beliefs. Basic beliefs could

---

24. See chapter 1 in Ayer, *Language Truth and Logic*, 13–29.

25. David Hugh Freeman, "Translator's Introduction," in Spier's *Christianity and Existentialism*, xii. Here Freeman argues that a "theoretical thought is based upon super-theoretical ideas and no pure unprejudiced reason exists." This is also the central thesis of the "new school of Christian philosophy" associated with its founder, Hermann Dooyeweerd.

26. See Plantinga, "Reason and Belief in God."

be a result of one's perception. For example, my belief that this rose is red is acquired immediately and not on the basis or support of any other belief. It is quite possible that I am wrong in my perception, depending on if I were color blind or suffered from a jaundiced eye. The point here is not which belief is true; rather, it is about how one's belief is obtained and sustained. Typically, perceptual beliefs are held without the support of other beliefs. My belief that the sun rose this morning is a basic belief. However, when I infer that I perceive the sun rising because of the earth's rotation on its axis, I have inferred it based on other beliefs and hence it is a non-basic belief. Therefore, there are beliefs that are non-basic, which are beliefs that are inferred or held by evidential support from other beliefs.

## Truth Discourse and Kierkegaardian Insights

Truth can be understood in two senses: one, in its original sense as fidelity entailing subjective appropriation; and two, as a state of being—the case or "fact" in an objective sense along the representation-correspondence views. Much of analytical philosophy sees truth merely in the objective sense, which would also require a God's-eye-view of things to know things as they really are. Although a God's-eye-view is impossible, truth discourses by default are undertaken in this sense. Consequently, truth discourses pertain to "what" it is. However, although truth discourse in this sense is inescapable, it nevertheless remains inconclusive. Even contemporary discussions—be it the Rortian understanding of truth as communal solidarity, Foucaultian truth connections with power, or Derrida's deconstruction of representational realism—all seem to touch upon something necessary, and yet each provides a far from satisfactory understanding of truth.

This inconclusiveness paves the way to recognize the futility of pursuing truth primarily in the objective sense of what it is, with no bearing on truth as subjectivity. Further, this inconclusiveness is an awareness of ignorance—a knowing that one does not know. It is this recognition that motivates Kierkegaard to raise the question of truth in a more authentic sense as fidelity, which he terms as subjectivity, to which I shall return later. This recognition is both Socratic (the recognition that one does not know) and non-Socratic (the recognition that truth has to be given from without). For Kierkegaard, this opens up a way to locate truth, contra Socrates, as from outside the individual and as given. When truth is given [revelation], one needs the ability to recognize it as truth [condition]. This requires not only that truth be given, but also that the condition for truth be given. For Kierkegaard, incarnation is that point when both are given. Kierkegaard's project is to see truth as fidelity to God, for that should be the right kind of pursuit. This is not to suggest that truth in an objective sense does not exist; but rather that human pursuit of truth should primarily be undertaken subjectively.

## On the (Im)possibility of a God's-Eye-View

Kierkegaard's thinking against an objective approach to truth is not that there is no such thing as objective truth. However, in the way that Hegel conceived objective truth, he eliminated inwardness, where, "for the sake of objectivity the knower abandons first person discourse and seeks to become impersonal, dispassionate, and disinterested—systematically and intentionally cut off from all existential questions and *a fortiori* from faith."[27] His target therefore, is not objectivity *per se*, but the type of objectivity that removed truth from being a personal concern. Nor is his target the representational nature of truth, as a representational or correspondence criterion can still be introduced into the Climacean purpose, where subjectivity can be evaluated against a standard set of values it stands for. The objection to speculative thought is not that it is a "false presupposition" but rather that it is a "comic presupposition occasioned by its having forgotten in a kind of world historical absent-mindedness, what it means to be a human being..."[28] Kierkegaard's target therefore, is the presumption that objective truth could be pursued in a dispassionate way as an impersonal observer with a God's-eye point of view. For Kierkegaard, Hegel epitomized such a dispassionate pursuit of truth.

Hegel (1770–1831) is the most prominent of the founders of Classical German Idealism, other important names being Johann Gottlieb Fichte and Friedrich Wilhelm Joseph Schelling. They tried to strip the concept of the unknowable "thing-in-itself" from the philosophy of Kant, thus bringing out a metaphysical idealism from Kant's critical idealism. Following Kant, these idealists began with formal consideration of knowledge, although they affirmed later that the absolute is recognized through an intuitive immediacy: moral for Fichte, aesthetic for Schelling, rational for Hegel.[29]

27. Westphal, "Kierkegaard and Hegel," 113.
28. CUP, 120.
29. See Thorslev, "German Romantic Idealism," 87.

## Truth and Subjectivity, Faith and History

Hegel exerted great influence on the history of philosophy (and eventually on the philosophy of history as well), the study of all social sciences, and indeed on some life sciences. The Hegelian system was the reigning philosophy between 1820 and 1840 and made inroads into every German university. Following Hegel's death, the school split into conservative and liberal parties. Opinions diverged upon matters such as God, Christ, immortality, etc., as Hegel had not expressed himself indubitably. While the conservatives interpreted the system in orthodox supernaturalistic terms—preserving theism, personal immortality, and an incarnate God—the liberals held to a spiritualistic pantheism—God is the universal substance, which becomes conscious in humankind.

Hegel countered Kant by arguing that there can be no unknowable "thing-in-itself"; rather, the content and the forms of knowledge are merely products of the mind. He concluded that all objects of knowledge, including things, are the products of the mind. Hegel argued that there was nothing unknowable, and felt that one could know the inner secrets of absolute reality. Accordingly, he said that absolute reality has to be some form of rationality because there is no independent and essentially unknowable external "thing-in-itself" that causes consciousness. For Hegel, every reality is rational and what is rational is real. Nature and mind, or reason for Hegel, are one, yet he subordinates nature to reason. Since reality is rational, and the function of logic is to understand the laws according to which reason operates, Hegel says, logic and metaphysics are one and the same. Therefore, all of historical reality, including human activity, follows the laws of thought. Philosophy accordingly, is in the business of knowing the world of nature and of human experience, their eternal essence, harmony, and law. All processes in the world follow a rational order.[30]

Hegelian speculation, argues Westphal, entailed "that the system must be presuppositionless and that it must be final. . . . In both cases the speculative philosopher needs to occupy a standpoint outside of time, and whether the eternity that must be achieved is represented as before or after time is not very important."[31] For Kierkegaard, Hegel's entire project begins with a flaw, in that sin is presupposed, on the one hand, and yet, on the other, a system achieving perfection is attempted. If sin is presupposed, the solution cannot be provided by a system that assumes a God's-eye-view, for such an assumption would be comparable to the Christian, who is depicted

---

30. Thilly, *A History of Philosophy*, 462–65.
31. Westphal, "Kierkegaard and Hegel," 119.

as worse off than the idolater, in the Climacean parable of the penitent idolater.[32] Where sin is presupposed, the only appropriate response would be that of penitence.

The speculative thinker's attempt to present his ideas as a dispassionate thinking of the whole is merely comical, as Climacus argues, "for an existing person pure thinking is a chimera when the truth is supposed to be the truth in which to exist."[33] Climacus' target here is the Hegelian and modernistic arrogance that pretends to avail a neutral view from nowhere in one's pursuit of truth. The greater culpability of modern Enlightenment thinking is in the fact that it is a form of Christendom—a subversion of Christianity. Be it Descartes or Hegel, pure thought was never an imagination of paganism but has always entirely been a product of Christendom. Climacus lays the central problem at human proclivity to counterfeit the Christian practice of mimesis with philosophical systems, and even more so, when it is done in the name of Christianity. Climacus assumes (and now the postmodernist assumes) that every individual works from a point of concrete givenness, rather than from a point that gives him the God's-eye point of view. Kierkegaard contends that any thinking must begin with the concrete individual.

The postmodern suspicion of truth-claims is understandable given the human propensity to exploit even the message of love and vulnerability of the cross for personal gain. A postmodern "radical" hermeneutics expectedly "cultivates an acute sense of the contingency of all social, historical, linguistic structures, an appreciation of their constituted character, their character as effects."[34] However, a Kierkegaardian acknowledgement of human contingency and constitutedness is not merely from a social-historical-linguistic perspective, but is based on human finitude and fallenness. In line with Augustinian thinking, Climacus argues that humans as created beings are, by nature, contingent. Kierkegaardian anthropology recognizes the Pauline caution about "all ungodliness and wickedness of men who by their wickedness suppress the truth."[35] However, for the same reason, the Kierkegaardian method rightly suspects not only the modernistic assumptions but also the arrogant postmodern denials of truth.

---

32. Chapter 3 will have a more detailed discussion on the parable of the penitent idolater.

33. CUP, 310.

34. Caputo, *Radical Hermeneutics*, 209.

35. Rom 1:18.

## Truth and Subjectivity, Faith and History

In his work *Overcoming Ontotheology*, Merold Westphal clarifies the postmodern understanding of truth by distinguishing between Truth with a capital T and truth. To understand the postmodern claim, "the truth is that there is no Truth,"[36] it is crucial to understand that what the postmodernists claim as impossible is "Truth" with a capital T, and not truth. Westphal thus argues that, within the givenness of human finitude, truth with no pretension to absoluteness is still possible. This should lead one neither to a relativism nor to an abandonment of reason.

Westphal uses the Kantian distinction between the noumenal (*das Ding an sich* or "thing-in-itself") and the phenomenal (*das Ding an sich* or "thing-as-it-appears") worlds to put things in perspective. This Kantian distinction, which became a precursor to postmodern anti-realism, argues Westphal, has often been misunderstood to mean a distinction between the real object and the unreal or object of appearance. However, a careful reading, suggests Westphal, "makes it clear that this is just a . . . way of speaking about two ways of apprehending one set of objects."[37] The Kantian distinction between the world of appearance and the thing-in-itself is a distinction between human, finite knowledge and divine, infinite knowledge. Kant was rather pessimistic about the possibility of human knowledge of the "true world," as humans could know things only as they appeared. Having used Kant sympathetically to peep into human helplessness, a condition for which most postmodern thinkers offer little help, we need to recognize the limits of the Kantian distinction itself. As Ingraffia argues, "Kant's true world is not only 'indemonstrable' and 'unattainable for now,' but also, unlike Christianity's true world, 'unpromisable.' . . . This philosophical belief in an unknown world, the thing-in-itself, results from the loss of belief in Christianity's divine world."[38]

Our worldviews emanate from particular vantage points and cannot claim to be a view outside the limits of space and time or as the alpha and omega points, which are purely God's prerogative. Although Kierkegaard is more suspicious of human reason than Kant is, Climacus implicitly finds an ally in the Kantian explication of the limits of reason. However, unlike Kant, Kierkegaard would not trust practical reason either, as he factors in the problem of sin. Once sin is factored in, a pursuit of truth is modified as

---

36. To understand how this statement is not the contradiction it is often made out to be, see Westphal, *Overcoming Ontotheology*, 85–86.

37. Ibid., 92.

38. Ingraffia, *Postmodern Theory and Biblical Theology*, 38.

a process of appropriation rather than as a finished product that is cognitively known. Thus, *subjectivity is truth!* Subjectivity is a "coming to be"—a continuous, ongoing process, which (as a continuous process) escapes conclusive apprehension.

In the postmodern milieu, the problem of truth raises the question, "whether it exists" and if it does, "whether it is accessible." Radical relativists and many postmodernists, in denying the very existence of Truth with a capital T, find it unnecessary to raise questions about its accessibility. Whereas, in the Kierkegaardian scheme, the inaccessibility of truth, unlike the relativists, assumes that there is Truth with a capital T, which however, is out of bounds for man because of his finitude and depravity. A contingent being cannot intrinsically possess truth but can only derive it from God. Climacus quotes Lessing approvingly to say: "If God held all truth enclosed in his right hand, and in his left hand the one and only ever-striving drive for truth, even with the corollary of erring forever and ever, and if he were to say to me: Choose!—I would humbly fall down to him at his left hand and say: Father, give! Pure truth is indeed only for You alone!"[39]

The question then would be, "how would one know that there is Truth with a capital T, if it is not accessible?" Further still, how can one know the existence of something that no human can possibly possess? Epistemologically, it is important to distinguish the stance that accentuates human finitude, while allowing for the possibility of the existence of Truth and a more arrogant postmodern stance that denies the very existence of Truth. The Kierkegaardian hermeneutic of finitude is, therefore, qualitatively different from the postmodern hermeneutics of suspicion. The former sees human finitude as a human condition in contradistinction to the absolute, while the latter sees the human condition itself as absolute. The relativistic reversal to absolutism becomes apparent, as a denial of absolute Truth, besides making an absolute claim that there is no absolute truth, also assumes infinite knowledge. Notably the affirmation of the existence of Truth with a capital T as properly belonging to God could very well function as a basic belief, whose epistemic status is based on faith. It could also very well function as any pre-theoretical commitment.

---

39. CUP, 106.

# Truth and Subjectivity, Faith and History

## Postmodern Suspicion and Kierkegaard's Hermeneutic of Finitude

Although Kierkegaard's hermeneutic of finitude and the postmodern hermeneutic of suspicion have to be clearly distinguished, it seems that a postmodern hermeneutic of suspicion is a natural successor to Kierkegaard's hermeneutic of finitude, where the human condition is a fallen one. As Westphal puts it, "Taken together, the hermeneutics of finitude and of suspicion tell us: We cannot attain to the Truth, and if we could, we would edit (that is, revise) it to suit our current agenda."[40]

Kierkegaardian anthropology and his objection to Hegel's speculative thought are grounded in the conception of man as contingent. First, man as contingent entails that no human has final truth. Second, the human claim for truth grounded in the autonomy of the human subject, could be suspected along the Lyotard-Foucaultian lines. As Westphal argues, the Kierkegaardian perspective is that the Christian narrative, "legitimizes only one kingdom, the kingdom of God. In the process, it delegitimizes every human kingdom, including democratic capitalism and the Christian church, just to the degree that they are not the full embodiment of God's kingdom. Modernity's metanarratives legitimize 'us'; the Christian narrative places 'us' under judgment as well."[41] In the Kierkegaardian schema, all human interests, even the best, are subject to adulteration because of his or her fallenness. For Climacus, "the knower is an existing person, and thus truth cannot be an identity for him as long as he exists."[42] Given human finitude and depravity, humans ought to pursue truth as: "An objective uncertainty, held fast through appropriation with the most passionate inwardness, is the truth, the highest truth there is for an existing person."[43]

C. S. Lewis' caution about the human penchant to swing from an error at one end of the spectrum to another at the opposite end is in place here. In dealing with the devil, he says, humans are either overly obsessed with the devil or entirely deny his existence. Kierkegaardian truth discourse addresses stalemates within the extremes of the absolutist, Enlightenment truth-claims and the relativist, postmodern truth-denials. Even Socratic irony transcended the inadequacy of these outlooks in presenting truth as exhibited in the form of the absolute good. Besides avoiding an overt

---

40. Westphal, *Overcoming Ontotheology*, 84.
41. Ibid., xv.
42. CUP, 196.
43. CUP, 203.

arrogance, the Socratic attempt lays the demands on the individual as superior to a community's accepted standards of morality, arrived at by mere solidarity and even, perhaps, the laws of the state. However, for Kierkegaard, Truth belongs to God, and any human encounter of it is possible only in the existing individual relating to the incarnated Christ.

## Procuring Truth

### Socrates and Christ Contrasted

Climacus draws a contrast between two divergent ways of reconciling eternal truth and the contingent historical context. One is Socratic, the other is Christian. The Socratic position is expounded by Plato in his *Meno*, where he wonders if one can really acquire any new knowledge. The story is that of a slave boy without schooling, who, when asked about a geometric problem, is able to arrive at the right answer with some prompting. With this, Socrates maintains that we already possess knowledge in the form of latent memory that can be brought to consciousness. The teacher only does the job of a midwife to bring out that which is already present within. If one already knows the truth, it cannot be pursued; if one does not know the truth, how can he identify it as truth when it is encountered? Either way, knowledge seems impracticable.[44] For Socrates, the answer is to become aware of the presence of truth within: "it was a matter of tapping or unlocking knowledge that was in some sense already there."[45] It is making explicit that which is implicit.

The best of the Pagan position, including most of the schools within the Indian philosophical traditions, locates the truth as already within the individual, as illustrated by Socrates. Climacus complains that the Socratic stance leads to an ordinariness of the truth and its encounter. The moment of truth would then be an "ordinary" moment; after all, it was always within the individual and could have been made explicit anytime. Furthermore, the teacher is also ordinary and is only an occasion to realize that which the student already knew. However, since truth must be eternal, Climacus wonders how the eternal truth could be contained in that ordinary moment of learning and how the ordinary teacher can articulate the eternal. An alternative to the Socratic approach means two things. First, since the

44. PF, 9. cf. Plato, *Meno*, 80d.
45. Gardiner, *Kierkegaard*, 69.

truth is external to us, it must be introduced to us from the outside. The progression here is not from the implicit to the explicit, but from without to within. Second, since we are bereft of the condition for obtaining the truth, there has to be an inward change so as to recognize it when encountered. He says, "Now, if the learner is to obtain the truth, the teacher must bring it to him, but not only that. Along with it, he must provide him with the condition for understanding it. . . . But no human being is capable of doing this; if it is to take place, it must be done by the God himself."[46]

By positing the individual as not only lacking truth, but also as one who does not even have the condition, Climacus affirms the total depravity of humans. Accordingly, since "all instruction depends upon the presence of the condition; if it is lacking, then a teacher is capable of nothing, because in the second case, the teacher, before beginning to teach, must transform, not reform, the learner."[47] In the section called "thought-project" in the *Fragments*, Climacus, by distinguishing the two possible ways of approaching truth, also builds the foundation to explicate the unique nature of the incarnation of Christ. In the next section titled "The God as Teacher and Savior (A Poetic Venture)," he explicates Christ as the teacher and giver of the condition. Climacus writes, "The teacher, then, is the god himself, who, acting as the occasion, prompts the learner to be reminded that he is untruth and is that through his own fault. But this state—to be untruth and to be that through one's own fault—what can we call it? Let us call it *sin*."[48] For Kierkegaard, the question of truth, ultimately, is really a question about salvation, which defines untruth as sin, unlike Socrates who defines it as ignorance.

## Divine and Human Agencies

How does Climacus reconcile the concept of faith both as something that the teacher bestows and as a human response? Does a "cat grip" (where the mother cat is in total control of every movement of the kitten) or a "monkey grip" (where a young baby monkey holds on to its mother) best represent the learner's role? Given the different uses of the term "faith," it would be difficult to conclusively say what Kierkegaard means by them. Pointing to a range of usage of the word "faith," Pojman writes:

46. PF, 14–15.
47. PF, 14.
48. PF, 15.

> Sometimes it seems to mean the capacity to believe; sometimes it seems to mean a knowledge of the truth. The word is sometimes used to describe the vision of God. It is a miracle which opens the "eyes of faith." Faith is contemporaneity with its object. It is the organ for apprehending the historical, and, in its eminent sense, the organ for apprehending the Eternal's appearance in history. It is "happy passion." It is a form of knowledge. It is an act of the will, a volition. It is not a form of knowledge.[49]

It may be interesting to note that, as a student, Kierkegaard was troubled with the problem of predestination or an extreme version of it called *supralapsarianism*.[50] He took pains to show that it violated the true nature of man's existence, while being careful of not falling into Pelagianism, the other extreme. Climacus maintains the dialectical tension in keeping both grace and human freedom as important without swaying to either extreme, which according to Pojman, is "a modified, synergistic version of Augustinianism in which freedom is paradoxically coupled with a notion of original sin and divine election."[51]

By way of holding the two views in dialectical tension, Climacus suggests a rather modest, yet concrete role for the individual in truth appropriation. It is to let go of what is naturally found in him, thus contributing *via negativa*, a resignation, to give up something, to let go of my trust in human reason, which Climacus says, "is, after all, *meine Zuthat* [my contribution]."[52] A further elaboration of personal accountability is given in Kierkegaard's *Journals and Papers*:

> In order to constrain subjectivity, we are quite properly taught that no one is saved by works, but by grace—and corresponding to that—by faith. Fine. But am I therefore unable to do something myself with regard to becoming a believer? Either we must answer this with an unconditional "no," and then we have fatalistic election by grace, or we must make a little concession. The point is this—subjectivity is always under suspicion, and when it is established that we are saved by faith, there is immediately the suspicion that

---

49. Pojman, *The Logic of Subjectivity*, 92.

50. Supralapsarianism is an extreme form of Calvinistic belief where God's predestination of some humans to eternal life and some others to damnation is seen as logically prior even to his act of creation.

51. Pojman, "Kierkegaard on Freedom," 142.

52. PF, 43.

> too much has been conceded here. So an addition is made: But no one can give himself faith; it is a gift of God I must pray for.
>
> Fine, but then I myself can pray, or must we go farther and say: No, praying (consequently praying for faith) is a gift of God which no man can give to himself; it must be given to him. And what then? Then to pray aright must again be given to me so that I may rightly pray for faith, etc.
>
> There are many, many envelopes—but there must still be one point or another where there is a halt at subjectivity. Making the scale so large, so difficult, can be commendable, as a majestic expression for God's infinity, but subjectivity cannot be excluded, unless we want to have fatalism.[53]

The individual also has another modest, yet positive task at hand—to accept the truth when the eternal presents himself before him, thus emphasizing the volitional act in believing. In the words of Climacus, "the eternal, essential truth is not behind him but has come in front of him by existing itself or by having existed, so that if the individual, existing, does not lay hold of the truth in existence, he will never have it."[54] Every individual then exists with the possibility of eternal life—a relationship with ideally "the eternal Christian God, but minimally to some other concept of the eternal."[55] However, if a learner cannot arrive at the truth by recollection, how does he appropriate the truth? What is the role of a learner? Climacus' treatment of divine grace and human responsibility provides an interesting perspective on the issue. Given the tendency to lean to either of the two extremes on the issue, the traditional attempts often accentuate one at the expense of the other. Quite consciously, Climacus lends himself to diverse interpretations. On the one hand, in keeping with the Augustinian tradition, he asserts that "faith is not an act of will,"[56] and the individual is at the mercy of the non-Socratic teacher, who not only gives the truth, but also provides the condition to receive it. On the other hand, he maintains that belief is "an act of freedom,"[57] emphasizing human responsibility. Mark C. Taylor goes so far as to write, "It is of central importance for Kierkegaard's

---

53. JP, 4:4551.
54. CUP, 209.
55. Watkin, *Kierkegaard*, 28.
56. PF, 62.
57. PF, 83.

argument that man himself be responsible for faith."⁵⁸ On interpreting Kierkegaard, Lee Barrett writes, "Some commentators applaud Climacus' profound emphasis of divine grace and his exposure of human incapacity apart from grace, two themes which have been central to the followers of Augustine. . . . Other commentators, however, have discovered in Climacus, and in Kierkegaard himself, an emphasis upon faith as an act of human autonomy which has affinities with Augustine's adversary Pelagius."⁵⁹

Since truth as given by God can be understood as salvation itself, we can ask the question, what does Climacus mean by "condition," which, he maintains, is also provided by God? According to Taylor's summary of Climacus' view, "God only provides the possibility of faith by presenting a possible object for faith, the incarnation, while human beings must freely decide to actualize this new possibility."⁶⁰ Understanding God primarily as the provider of the *possibility* of faith still turns the weight of procuring or actualizing it upon the individual.

However Climacus, in explicating his idea of the "condition for faith," seems to think that humans need more help than just the possibility of faith. He presupposes that the depravity of humans has alienated them to the extent that there is nothing in them that could facilitate, let alone, initiate faith. Thus an individual, with all the force of reason, strength of will and the weight of passion together, cannot accomplish anything that could credit himself as having caused his own transformation. Furthermore, he can credit neither himself nor his tradition or the church or someone else who could have provided an occasion to encounter the truth as he "is not indebted to someone else for something but is indebted to the god for everything."⁶¹ In articulating God as the sole agent for salvation, Climacus also implies that the condition provided is not something that is already available in some general way to all humanity, either in the way their noetic structure is wired or through a general revelation. If it were the case, the Socratic teacher is made capable of teaching, as the condition is already present and no transformation would be required to cause learning. Rather the work of God in each individual is repeated throughout time, to cause a personal transformation into truth. The transformation is effected by a sin-consciousness. The imparting of the condition by the eternal teacher

58. Taylor, *Kierkegaard's Pseudonymous Authorship*, 314.
59. Barrett, "The Paradox of Faith," 262.
60. Ibid., 262.
61. PF, 102.

"prompts the learner to be reminded that he is untruth and is that through his own fault. Nevertheless, this state—to be untruth and to be that through one's own fault—what can we call it? Let us call it *sin*."[62] In line with Paul's idea of the "new creature," Climacus conceives the condition to be a new nature that is bestowed by a transformation of the existing individual. According to Climacus, "As a result of receiving the condition in the moment, his course [of life] took the opposite direction, or he was turned around."[63] It is in the nature of the old self to not recognize, reject or even ridicule faith. Thus, the one who has obtained the condition has simultaneously also obtained a new self in the place of the old, with the new one suggesting, "a new set of concerns, passions, attitudes, and aspirations discontinuous with the individual's old patterns of emotion, valuation, and action."[64]

The condition that is given by the divine teacher thus involves both sin-consciousness and truth-awareness, which function together as two sides of a coin. Defining paganism as being "without God in the world," Anti-Climacus, Kierkegaard's Christian pseudonym, writes, "Therefore, from another point of view, it is true that in the strictest sense the pagan did not sin, for he did not sin before God, and all sin is before God."[65] Sin-consciousness is not possible outside Christianity and is surely not something that is granted via human reasoning or general revelation, but is divinely granted as a condition with truth-awareness. "The concept of sin" for Anti-Climacus, is what "most decisively differentiates Christianity qualitatively from paganism, and this is also why Christianity very consistently assumes that neither paganism nor the natural man knows what sin is; in fact, it assumes that there has to be a revelation from God to show what sin is."[66] Accordingly, although truth-awareness (of which sin-consciousness is a part) may involve affirmation of certain beliefs that can be explicated as doctrines or propositions, it is primarily granted rather than willed.

Climacus suggests that volition finds its positive role only after the condition is given. He writes, "It is easy to see, then (if, incidentally, the consequences of discharging the understanding need to be pointed out), that faith is not an act of will, for it is always the case that all human willing

---

62. PF, 15.
63. PF, 13.
64. Barrett, "The Paradox of Faith," 273.
65. SUD, 81.
66. SUD, 89.

is efficacious only within the condition."[67] Echoing the Augustinian idea of the fallen will as intrinsically incapable of right action, Climacus sees the necessity for the condition to be effected prior to the human willing for it to be efficacious. Conversely, any human willing without the condition merely remains ineffective at its best or demonstrates human arrogance at its worst. The human task is nevertheless not abolished in the Climacean understanding. He writes, "By Baptism, Christianity gives him a name, and he is a Christian *de nomine*; but in the decision he becomes a Christian and gives Christianity his name (*nomen dare alicui* [to give a name to someone])."[68] Although becoming a Christian is purely by grace, it seems to involve a basic awareness of Christianity's radical demands on the individual and a commitment to it. Once the condition is given by virtue of the new self, the tasks required of it is correspondingly higher, as the parable of the penitent idolater in *Concluding Unscientific Postscript* implies.[69] Thus, Kierkegaard holds the biblical truism, "Every one to whom much is given, of him will much be required; and of him to whom men commit much they will demand the more."[70]

If faith and the condition for faith are given and not acquired by an act of will, then, how do we understand Climacus' seemingly contrasting statement, that "belief is not a knowledge but an act of freedom, an expression of will"?[71] Apart from the immediate dislocation of belief (in Danish *Troen* is used for both faith and belief) from a purely cognitive construal of faith as knowing certain doctrinal concepts, Climacus seeks to imply a nuanced notion of freedom. True freedom that was lost with the fall of the first Adam is now granted as a condition by the last Adam. Freedom, rightly understood, is not just the ability to choose, but is the ability to choose right—an ability that is lost through sin that entails a futility of human volition outside the condition. It is at the moment of the incarnation of Christ, both a historical advent and more so a personal advent in the individual's moment of faith, that freedom is received again as a condition. Thus, faith becomes both an act of freedom and an expression of will. As in his *Journals*, Kierkegaard records that "faith certainly requires an expression of will, and yet in another sense than when, for example, I must say that all

67. PF, 62.
68. CUP, 373.
69. CUP, 201.
70. Luke 12:48.
71. PF, 83.

cognition requires an expression of will; how else can I explain the passage in the New Testament which says that he who does not have faith shall be punished."[72] Climacus recognizes the contradiction involved in talking of faith as caused by freedom, which itself is caused at the moment of faith. He writes, "But the contradiction is that he receives the condition in the moment, and, since it is a condition for the understanding of eternal truth, it is *eo ipso* the eternal condition. If this is not the structure, then we are left with Socratic recollection."[73] "But once the condition is bestowed," writes Emmanuel, "the God-man becomes, by his example, the occasion for the learner to be 'reminded that he is untruth' in this way, he is very much like the Socratic midwife."[74]

## Religious Doctrine and Its Role

Doctrines are an essential part of the Christian faith. Contrary to most religious faiths where salvation is seen as a result of obedience to a law, Christianity sees it as resulting from faith. What constitutes faith therefore becomes a question of greater importance for Christianity than for other religions. The connection between faith and doctrinal beliefs undoubtedly accentuates the value of its doctrine in Christianity. If one's belief counts for much, it is natural for a believer to examine the content of his beliefs to ensure he believes what is true. Further, Christian growth presupposes the deepening of our understanding of reality as taught in the Scriptures.

How then should one understand Kierkegaard's purpose of infusing the truth of Christianity into Christendom and his clear downplaying of Christian doctrines? Does it imply a negation of doctrine or its insignificance for Christianity? In the *Journals* Kierkegaard complains about what is perceived to be true Christianity. He writes, "As soon as I take Christianity as a doctrine and then apply my acumen or my profundity or my eloquence or my imagination to presenting it, people think it is fine and I am regarded as an earnest Christian, I am esteemed, etc. As soon as I will express existentially [existentielt] what I say, consequently situate Christianity in

---

72. JP, 2:1094. Cf. Rom 14:23, which reads, "for whatever does not proceed from faith is sin."

73. PF, 62.

74. Emmanuel, *Kierkegaard and the Concept of Revelation*, 69.

actuality—then it is exactly as if I had blown up the world. People are immediately scandalized."[75]

Kierkegaard affirms the doctrinal content albeit only in connection with the intended purpose of the doctrine, which is personal transformation. What is negated is the equivocation of Christianity with a purely propositional consideration of doctrine. When doctrine is conceived as a proposition, what is tested for correctness is the doctrine, not the self. At the centre of such an approach is neither God nor the self. On the correctness of the doctrine, theologians can lose their sleep. However, Kierkegaard would rather have an individual lose sleep over one's own struggle to become authentic. In Christianity one encounters the truth not primarily as a set of doctrines but as the very person of God encountering the subject. It is this accent on the personal nature of doctrine that emphasizes the *how* of faith rather than the *what*. Yet, Climacus also acknowledges that when the *how* is appropriated, the *what* is also given. The modern accent on the cognitive extrapolations of the Bible and Christian doctrines is in a manner that can be totally dissociated from one's personal life. It is Kierkegaard's rejection of such a dichotomy that defines his approach as fundamentally against a purely cognitive appropriation of the doctrines. Further, even when he argues for a relationship, it is not to be assumed as a knowledge-centered relationship where Christ is seen as one who teaches a doctrine because this would again make the doctrine a matter of greater interest.[76] This should inform us of the true meaning of Climacus' statement, "Christianity is not a doctrine, but it expresses an existence-contradiction and is an existence-communication."[77]

Arguing for Kierkegaard's "functional approach to doctrine," Gouwens writes, "'Meaning' and 'truth' in Christian faith are not located in the doctrines themselves or conveyed by them as such, but are found only in the life within which the doctrines are used."[78] It is in paganism that truth is equated with a doctrine or principle, which is greater than the individual. Christianity is unlike any religion or philosophy where the principle or the system becomes more important than the individual. This unparalleled value given to each individual is uniquely Christian and is noticed repeatedly in the New Testament. Just as the "prodigal son's father waited, or he

---

75. JP, 1:511.
76. Henriksen, *The Reconstruction of Religion*, 114.
77. CUP, 379–80, 570.
78. Gouwens, "Kierkegaard's Understanding of Doctrine," 17.

does not stand and wait, he goes to seek the sinner as the shepherd sought the strayed sheep.... Indeed, he walked the infinitely long way from being God to becoming man; he walked that way in order to seek sinners."[79] An individual who is thus sought and encountered by God can only respond to it. He cannot define truth nor fully comprehend it, but can nevertheless relate and belong to God who is the truth. In other words, the individual does not comprehend the truth, but rather is apprehended by the truth.

Similarly, in Christianity, along with the maximal value accorded to the individual, a corresponding maximal value is accorded to the incarnated Christ. In every other philosophy or religion, the founder is conceived as just an occasion or a bearer of truth. There is nothing that ties the founder or his life with the doctrine he teaches, in that it is conceivable that someone else could have delivered the same message or teaching. The teaching therefore becomes more important than the teacher. However, in Christianity the opposite is true because the God-man himself is the truth. There is a conflation of Christ as both the messenger and the message because "the Word became flesh and dwelt among us, full of grace and truth."[80] Thus Anti-Climacus writes that Christ is, "infinitely more important than his teaching. It is true only of a human being that his teaching is more important than he himself; to apply this to Christ is a blasphemy, inasmuch as it makes him into only a human being."[81] Kierkegaardian response should then be rightly understood in the context of the priority accorded to the personage, both the individual and the God-man, over doctrines.

Furthermore, Kierkegaard's defining Christianity as not a doctrine also ought to be understood in the context of many a theologian's preoccupation with the doctrine, often at the expense of a similar concern to align one's life in accordance to Christ's teaching. This preoccupation provides a form of religion or a semblance of religiosity where one is "looked upon as a serious Christian" while remaining far from the heart of Christianity. This contradiction is inherent in the job description of every theologian, in that the time or effort in explicating every theological doctrine does not in itself accomplish the true purpose of Christ's teachings to transform the soul. The nineteenth-century developments that sought to reconcile the higher criticisms based on Enlightenment thinking with traditional protestant orthodoxy further heightened this problem. Accordingly, Schleiermacher

79. PC, 20.
80. John 1:14.
81. PC, 124.

defines doctrines as "accounts of the Christian religious affections set forth in speech."[82] This not only confines doctrine to accounts of speech, but also regulates the entire doctrine within the logico-semantic discourse. Such a prioritizing necessitated that a theologian harness all his resources to make an adequate articulation of doctrinal teachings, resulting in further elevation of logic and language as vehicles for transmitting truth, to the extent that truth and justification were confused. No matter how great the theological justification of a doctrine, it can never be conflated with truth. A logico-semantic priority in faith-discourses goes against the spirit of incarnation where the *Word became flesh* and tends to retain the Word as *Logos*. This type of logo-centrism, while accentuating the propositional nature of truth, does not really consider the significance of the Word becoming flesh, thus making it personal.

If the Enlightenment framework hijacked "faith" to mean rationally conceptualized belief systems, the postmodern counterparts also identify religious faith merely as cultural and linguistic expressions or as a "language-game," where a particular set of rules function within the limited sphere of the game in which it is employed. Both render the doctrine powerless to cause transformation. While the former uses the process of rationalizing to evade faith, the latter does so by its radical relativism. According to Steven Emmanuel, the analogy between language and doctrine explicates the Kierkegaardian understanding of religion. He writes, "just as there is a difference between knowing the rules of English grammar and *being* an English speaker, so is there also a difference between knowing the doctrines of Christianity and *being* Christian."[83]

It would then be misleading to compare Kierkegaard's account of faith with a theory that reduces it to a type of cultural or linguistic practice, where communities are seen as arbitrarily establishing the validity of the grammar and practice of faith. While such a comparison seeks to give a descriptive account of religious practice, it fails to articulate the uniqueness of the Christian faith, where one's *subjectivity* is a result of an individual's encounter with the incarnated Christ, irrespective of one's socio-cultural context. In so failing, it reduces Christianity to merely the form of a periodic social gathering of a community where the common beliefs provide

---

82. Schleiermacher, *The Christian Faith*, 76.

83. Emmanuel, "Kierkegaard On Doctrine," 364. Emmanuel also points out that Kierkegaard's view of religious doctrine is similar to George Lindbeck's "regulative" theory of doctrine.

the matrix for the functioning of the community, something akin to the Rortian ethnocentric scheme.

Conversely, for Kierkegaard, faith of the Abrahamic pattern carries an essential incommunicability and thus lies outside the universal and moral categories within a sociocultural context. This is not to imply that every instance of faith should carry with it the character of incommunicability, but rather that faith is ultimately manifest within categories that do not merely replicate social or cultural practices. Johannes de Silentio [John the Silent] draws a parallel between two instances of the practice of silence arising out of the incommunicability of the faith: Abraham's sacrifice of Isaac and Mary's extraordinary conception. He writes, "The angel was indeed a ministering spirit, but he was not a meddlesome spirit who went to the other young maidens in Israel and said: Do not scorn Mary, the extraordinary is happening to her. The angel went only to Mary, and no one could understand her."[84] Again, a reason why faith cannot be seen as an instance of arbitrary practice of religious language and grammar is precisely that, within the Kierkegaardian calculus, truth is located outside the individual and by implication, outside the community.

Drawing a contrast between Nietzsche, who critiqued Christianity from the "outside," and Kierkegaard, Calvin O. Schrag observes, "Kierkegaard forges his attack from the 'inside,' striving desperately to become a Christian in Christendom—or indeed *in spite of* Christendom!"[85] While linguistic and cultural interpretation has to do with philosophy of religion, Kierkegaard's focus was Christianity. If the former holds that logic is an arbitrary construction and it is perfectly conceivable that we should have employed different linguistic conventions, for Kierkegaard, faith ought to be based on the revelation of Christ and no arbitrary construction of belief system is imaginable. This difference, in essence, is the transition from religiousness A to religiousness B. "In religiousness A the movement is from self to God, finding God in the depths of the self. In the religiousness B the movement is from God to the self."[86] Kierkegaard writes, "In Religiousness B, the upbuilding is something outside the individual; the individual does not find the upbuilding by finding the relationship with God within himself, but relates himself to something outside himself to find the upbuilding."[87]

84. FT, 65.
85. Schrag, "The Kierkegaard-Effect," 9.
86. Ibid., 10.
87. CUP, 561.

As Calvin O. Schrag rightly says, "religiousness A . . . delineates the space for religion as a culture-sphere situated alongside or in dialectical relation with ethics and aesthetics as complementing culture-spheres, religiousness B is properly speaking, *not a culture-sphere at all*."[88] While a discussion on doctrine within culture-spheres could find a place within the religiousness A, Kierkegaard was opposed to constructing a type of Christianity on the basis of a common cultural form.[89] The only commonness in religiousness B is the acknowledgement that the entire humanity is placed within a common sphere of despair. For Kierkegaard, Christian doctrine cannot be considered apart from its teacher, the God-man/Christ, as if it was a subject to be learned rather than a way of life to be followed. While doctrines definitely have their place, for Kierkegaard, the imitation of Christ takes precedence over comprehension of doctrines, as a fixation with doctrines can become a way of distraction from imitation.

## Conclusion

An objective approach to understanding truth has its limits and in a Kierkegaardian sense, it is impossible to acquire a God's-eye-view of reality. Unlike the postmodern discourses, Kierkegaard locates the reasons for the impossibility of objective truth in the very nature of human self. The depravity or fallenness not only makes humans devoid of truth, but also renders human truth-pursuits, futile. Having typified all human truth-pursuits within the Socratic scheme, which essentially locates truth within the individual, Kierkegaard illustrates that truth has to be given from without. The God-man, through the moment of incarnation, makes the transcendent truth, immanent. Yet, Kierkegaard cautions against the greater trapping in reducing the knowledge of the God-man to a cognitive appropriation of Christian doctrines. Thus Climacus sums it up in the *Postscript*, "The difficulty is not to understand what Christianity is but to become and to be a Christian."[90]

---

88. Schrag, "The Kierkegaard-Effect," 11.
89. Henriksen, *The Reconstruction of Religion*, 112.
90. CUP, 560.

# 2

## Truthing through Subjectivity

*Of what use would it be to me for truth to stand before me, cold and naked, not caring whether or not I acknowledged it, making me uneasy rather than trustingly receptive. The crucial thing is to find a truth that is truth for me, to find the idea for which I am willing to live and die.* — JOURNALS AND PAPERS, 1835 (ENTRY OF AUGUST 1ST)

PARALLEL TO THE CONTOURS of human understandings of truth are corresponding understandings of the self, as the concepts of truth and self inform each other. Following René Descartes—the seventeenth-century rationalist, famous for his celebrated dictum, "I think, therefore I am"—the self as the autonomous agent of thought and knowledge acquired the central position. Known as the age of reason and embellished by scientific feats and discoveries, the eighteenth and nineteenth centuries witnessed great optimism regarding human capability. Drawing the difference between the pre-modern and the modern self, Charles Taylor writes, "The modern subject is self-defining, where on previous views the subject is defined in relation to a cosmic order."[1] Thus, the modern self defined itself, autonomously devoid of any reference to either a transcendent or a cosmic order, actualizing the Protagorian doctrine, "Man is the measure of all things."

---

1. Taylor, *Hegel*, 6.

In contrast, in postmodernity we observe that a general pessimism spans across environmental and geopolitical concerns, moral and social landscapes, and individual purpose and meaning of life. A sense of optimism concerning human capabilities has paved the way to pessimism. Removed from its seat of knowledge, value, and decision, the postmodern self exists in a state of flux. The postmodern mood is captured best by William Butler Yeats in his poem *The Second Coming*, "Things fall apart; the centre cannot hold; Mere anarchy is loosed upon the world."

Yet, one can notice the self-defining feature of the modern self that eliminates a transcendent point of reference persisting in the postmodern subject. Between the understanding of the self with all its pretentiousness as elevated and autonomous in modernity and a radically relativized self that is in a state of flux in postmodernity, insights from Kierkegaard can be drawn for a balanced view of the human self. Kierkegaard's reconstructive analysis in understanding self as an unfinished entity that is in a process of becoming provides a biblical alternative to the modern arrogant view of the self. Likewise, in understanding the self as anchored in a God-relation that establishes it, Kierkegaard avoids an entirely relativized postmodern view of self and a nihilism that this could entail.

## The Nature of the Self

Although, Kierkegaard's primary goal is not anthropological, his theological motifs are underpinned by anthropological assumptions. Kierkegaard recognizes his "present age" as "an age of disintegration,"[2] thus requiring remedial attention. A Kierkegaardian focus on the age of disintegration is not just a commentary on the rationalistic trends in the Denmark of his day but rather a description of any age that erects hurdles to faith via human arrogance or pretensions to know the truth. The way of redemption through the religious step can be circumvented not only by those who are committed to Hegel's elaborate speculative system but also by any philosophy or anti-philosophy that is propped up as an alternative to a passionate religious inwardness.

One becomes conscious of one's own self as a reflexive awareness, as Ishrat Jahan writes, "self constitutes the existential locus of a person, to focus on selves is then to direct observation on the experiencing, self-aware

---

2. PV, 119. He was also not optimistic of what would "become the future of history." See PV, 278.

human beings. Self-hood entails reflexive awareness, the recognition of oneself as an 'object in a world of objects.'"[3] The importance of the Socratic dictum, *know thyself*, cannot be over-emphasized in that one's understanding of the self, whether as the possessor of truth or as one without it, functions as an end [*telos*] unto itself. In a journal entry, Kierkegaard writes, "Life can only be understood backwards; but it must be lived forwards."[4] This entails that the self not only begins with a reflexive awareness of a self-definition that functions as *telos* but must also be actualized by an ethical commitment to live by that understanding. This seems to involve passional reflection, cognitive self-definition, and volitional commitment. In *The Sickness unto Death*, Anti-Climacus identifies a dialectical relation between the consciousness and the will of the human self. He writes: "Thus, consciousness is decisive. Generally speaking, consciousness—that is, self-consciousness—is decisive with regard to the self. The more consciousness, the more self; the more consciousness, the more will; the more will, the more self. A person who has no will at all is not a self; but the more will he has, the more self-consciousness he has also."[5]

This emphasis on the will is perhaps what motivates thinkers like Charles Taylor and Jacques Derrida to locate choice as the primary constituter of the self. Taylor, in *Sources of the Self* writes, "In choosing myself, I become what I really am, a self with an infinite dimension. We choose our real selves; we become for the first time true selves."[6] Likewise, Derrida talking about Abraham in *Fear and Trembling*, states, "Abraham's decision is absolutely responsible because it answers for itself before the absolute other."[7] However, given the overarching biblical view in Kierkegaard, choice as the primary constituter of the self needs to be understood within the purview of that choice being directed toward or away from a God-relation. In other words, it is not *any* choice that defines the self but the choice that pertains to God as its constituter. The Pauline anthropology that Kierkegaard presupposes sees only two options. In his letter to the Romans, Paul writes, "Do you not know that if you yield yourselves to any one as obedient slaves, you are slaves to the one whom you obey, either of sin, which leads to death,

---

3. Jahan, "The Social Construction of 'self'," 41.
4. JP, 1:1030, 1:1025.
5. SUD, 29.
6. Taylor, *Sources of the Self*, 450.
7. Derrida, *The Gift of Death*, 77.

or of obedience, which leads to righteousness?"[8] Paul alludes to both choice and slavery as a double condition of the human self, where one is already a slave to sin and only divine grace can free an individual, where freedom is maintained by obedience to Christ. Thus, one is always a slave—either to the self (sin) or to God (righteousness).

The Christian self is constituted not so much by the individual choices that are credited to the self, as by an enabling of the Spirit,[9] initiated at the moment of faith that results in an ontologically different self. In Pauline terms, the self in Christ becomes "a new creation."[10] Thus, the self is constituted not only by the exercise of the human will as a volitional agent but also by yielding to God. Such a choice is a choice against itself. Given that the self is constituted especially by its choice in relation to God, it is crucial to recognize that Kierkegaard's emphasis on the will not only shifts the entire weight of procuring both the truth and the condition for truth upon God as the dispenser of both but also makes human will culpable in the acts of self-deception. Such a thinking, which minimizes the role of the human will in procuring of the truth (salvation) and maximizes its culpability in self-deception, follows an Augustinian doctrine of bondage of the will and human depravity, whereby "people are free to sin but not free not to sin."[11]

Kierkegaard recognizes the full extent of human depravity and the complete fallenness of the self—the intellect, will, and passion—and the consequent human proclivity for self-deception. Echoing the prophetic warning, "The heart is deceitful above all things and beyond cure. Who can understand it?"[12] Kierkegaard recommends, "There is only one whom a person should fear, and that is God; and there is only one of whom a person should be afraid, and that is oneself."[13] The combined power of the fallen human soul—the rational, volitional, and passional faculties—arms the individual with exceptional ability for self-deception. The danger of self-deception does not diminish for the religiously inclined. In fact, they are at a greater risk. After all, the religious leaders of Jesus' time were the ones most deceived! Those who think they know are perhaps those who are truly deceived. The grip of self-deception is vicious precisely because of its very

---

8. Rom 6:16.
9. See chapter 6, for Kierkegaard's pneumatological insights.
10. 2 Cor 5:17.
11. Olson, *The Story of Christian Theology*, 273.
12. Jer 17:9.
13. WL, 15.

nature, where the self believes what it is not and does not believe what it is. Without resorting to the traditionalist method of convicting the flesh (*sarx*) and exonerating the soul (*psyche*), Kierkegaard locates the problem with the human soul as comprising *feeling, knowing, and willing—the affective, cognitive, and volitional* faculties. Anti-Climacus, Kierkegaard's Christian pseudonym, astutely traces the contours of self-deception in *The Sickness unto Death*. He writes:

> If a person does not do what is right at the very second he knows it—then, first of all, knowing simmers down. Next comes the question of how willing appraises what is known. Willing is dialectical and has under it the entire lower nature of man. If willing does not agree with what is known, then it does not necessarily follow that willingness goes ahead and does the opposite of what knowing understood (presumably such strong opposites are rare); rather, willing allows some time to elapse, an interim called: "we shall look at it tomorrow." During all this, knowing becomes more and more obscure, and the lower nature gains the upper hand more and more; alas, for the good must be done immediately, as soon as it is known . . . , but the lower nature's power lies in stretching things out. Gradually, willing's objection to this development lessens; it almost appears to be in collusion. And when knowing has become duly obscured, and knowing and willing can better understand each other; eventually they agree completely, for now knowing has come over to the other side of willing and admits that what it wants is absolutely right. And this is perhaps how great majority of men live; they work gradually at eclipsing their ethical and ethical-religious comprehension, which would lead them out into decisions and conclusions that their lower nature does not much care for, but they expand their esthetic and metaphysical comprehension, which ethically is a diversion.[14]

In the above passage, Anti-Climacus maps the dialectic between the rational and the volitional facets where the rational, via an interim, reasons on behalf of the will. An individual's obscuring of the knowing and its eventual collusion with the willing makes self-deception almost impossible to rid by self-effort. Echoing the Psalmist's prayer, "Search me, O God, and know my heart; Try me and know my thoughts,"[15] Kierkegaard thinks it prudent to be suspicious of one's affections and reasoning ability.

---

14. SUD, 94.
15. Ps 139:23.

## Truth and Subjectivity

### The Task of Becoming Subjective

Truth, for Kierkegaard, is subjectivity. By this, he does not mean that truth is subjectivism, where the individual is free to believe anything he wants without being plagued by the possibility of being in the wrong. Merold Westphal rightly argues that the synonym for subjectivity is not "subjectivism" or "arbitrariness," but "inwardness."[16] Far from advocating any kind of relativism, Kierkegaard uses the term *subjective* to turn the focus onto the subject. According to Malantschuk, the Kierkegaardian dictum *truth is subjectivity* "means simply that a man tries to act in accordance with the eternal truth which he finds in his innermost being. In this way the Eternal, which was only an abstract knowledge, acquires a personal meaning for a man."[17] Further, since truth is given from without by Christ, the absolute teacher, there is no possibility of truth being understood as subjectivism or arbitrariness. Thus, Kierkegaard is not to be misconstrued as saying, "it does not matter what one believes, as long as one is sincere." Conversely, for Socrates, as truth is located within the individual, "every human being is himself the midpoint, and the whole world focuses only on him because his self-knowledge is God-knowledge."[18] However, despite locating the truth within an individual, Socrates never meant it to mean some sort of arbitration.

The term "subjectivity" in Kierkegaard's writings does not signify one thing but a network of things, that connect related concepts such as inwardness, self-reflection, passion, will, emotions, etc. Climacus uses the concept of subjectivity to contrast abstract speculation, where one explores the realm of possibilities by means of rational techniques and attains only a hypothetical knowledge. Even where greater certitude is possible as in the case of mathematical truths, the question would be, what is in it for the individual? Subjectivity can therefore be understood as involving an inclination of the heart, which according to biblical imagery, is the wellspring of life.[19] As Pojman writes, "Every instance of subjectivity involves the will, though every act of the will need not involve subjectivity. Subjectivity may

---

16. Westphal, "Kierkegaard and Hegel," 112.
17. Malantschuk, *Kierkegaard's Way to the Truth*, 44.
18. PF, 11.
19. Prov 4:23.

be a sub-category of the will's activities, having to do with only those activities perceived to be vital to the spiritual life."[20] Thus, subjectivity cannot be construed as a metaphysical system but ought to be thought of as an approach that signifies the individual's self-involvement.

"Objectivity," on the other hand, "stands for a composite of attitudes, including unemotionality, disinterested evaluation, neutrality, impartial judgment, which leaves the interested subject out of the scene, and consensus, based on the public's assessment of the situation."[21] Climacus' complaint against the objective pursuit of truth is that its disinterested approach (dissociation from the self) entails no self-development and is thus practically useless for the individual. The speculative thought immersed in the pursuit of the objective, world-historical, according to Climacus, does "change him into something totally different in order to understand him. Nevertheless, what it is to live I cannot learn from him as someone dead and gone. I must experience that by myself, and therefore I must understand myself, not the reverse: after first having world-historically misunderstood him now go further and allow this misunderstanding to help me misunderstand myself, as if I, too, were dead and gone."[22]

Further contrasting the objective and subjective reflections in *Concluding Unscientific Postscript* Climacus explains, "To objective reflection, truth becomes something objective, an object, and the point is to disregard the subject. To subjective reflection, truth becomes appropriation, inwardness, subjectivity, and the point is to immerse oneself, existing, in subjectivity."[23] When the individual presumes to see the world as *sub specie aeterni* [from the viewpoint of eternity], he forgets that he is unlike God. Further, viewing the world as *sub specie aeterni*, the observer, "loses passion, and in return, truth does not become a paradox; but the knowing subject shifts from being human to being a fantastical something, and truth becomes a fantastical object for its knowing."[24] For Climacus, the distinction between the objective and subjective reflections is one of emphasis. "Objectively the emphasis is on *what* is said; subjectively the emphasis is on *how* it is said."[25] The former is interested only in categories of thought; while

20. Pojman, *The Logic of Subjectivity*, 55.
21. Ibid., 57.
22. CUP, 146–47.
23. CUP, 92.
24. CUP, 199.
25. CUP, 202.

*Truthing through Subjectivity*

the latter is interested in inwardness, which "is the passion of the infinite, and the passion of the infinite is the very truth."[26]

While considering Climacus' distinction of the objective and subjective approaches to truth, one should take into consideration the overall purpose of his works. His intention is not really to convince the reader of the *what* of the Christian faith. The objective content of the Christian beliefs was generally known and understood as true in his Danish context and thus required no further justification. What were missing though were a passionate inwardness and a subjective commitment to the Christian faith. It was indeed for the one who claimed to be a Christian that the Kierkegaardian calculus created a problem, for the knowledge of the incarnated God-man demands something more than a mental assent to certain creedal doctrines. It demands passion, inwardness, and earnestness, the absence of which amounts to a condition which Climacus alludes to in his parable of the penitent idolater—the Christian praying insincerely to the true god, which is worse than the prayer of an idolater who prays to an idol with true devotion.[27]

It therefore becomes pivotal to prevent one "from theorizing, even in an 'existential' sense about Christianity, and instead to help him to come to grips, in the isolation of his own subjectivity, with the question of what it means to become a Christian."[28] The question could be asked, "If passion is so pivotal, what about a genuine passion for abstract thought?" Climacean anthropology, which defines humans relationally, sees it as a self-contradiction, and Christianly speaking, idolatry, for a passionate relation rightly belongs to God and not to an abstract thought. Therefore, a genuine passion is possible only as far as an individual relates to another self and not to concepts or ideas, which are approximations. By contradiction, he means the individual appears comical in positing an absolute relation to a concept or an idea, as it lacks self-concern. Any theory that seeks to explain everything but lacks self-concern amounts to self-contradiction as it contradicts the self.[29]

A Climacean perspective of Nietzsche's *Thus Spake Zarathustra* would be interesting here. In it, the madman who looks for God and asks incessantly, "where is God?," partly taking the blame upon himself for the death

26. CUP, 203.
27. CUP, 201. This concept is further elaborated upon in chapter 3.
28. Allison, "Christianity and Nonsense," 290.
29. CUP, 31.

of god, declares that god is dead and can smell the stench. However, for Climacus, it appears that those standing around with their educated smiles would be farther from truth than the madman himself. He is mad from their perspective, primarily because God is a passionate issue for him, whereas for them, God has ceased to be an issue. In this sense, it is really those with the educated smiles for whom God is dead, as there is no passion for God in them.

Kierkegaard merely wants to labor the point that an objective approach is the way away from truth. Therefore, when Pontius Pilate objectified truth, he lost it and put Truth to death. Climacus writes, "If Pilate had not asked objectively what truth is, he would never have let Christ be crucified. If he had asked the question subjectively, then the passion of inwardness regarding *what he in truth had to do* about the decision facing him would have prevented him from doing an injustice."[30] Therefore, in as much as the objective approach to Christianity averts a passionately inward relation to God, it is not only useless, but also damaging to the self. In *Practice in Christianity*, Anti-Climacus, with Kierkegaard as the editor, affirms this idea as he reflects on Pilate's question, "What is truth?" He writes:

> Not as if he did not know what truth is; but when one is the truth and when the requirement is to be truth, to know the truth is an untruth. For knowing the truth is something that entirely of itself accompanies being the truth, not the other way around. And that is why it becomes untruth when knowing the truth is separated from being the truth or when knowing the truth is made identical with being it, since it is related the other way. Being the truth is identical with knowing the truth, and Christ would never have known the truth if he had not been it, and nobody knows more of the truth than what he is of the truth. . . . In other words, knowledge is related to the truth, but in the meantime I am untruthfully outside myself. The truth is within me, that is, when I am truly within myself (not untruthfully outside myself), the truth, if it is there, is a being, a *life*. Therefore it says, "This is eternal *life*, to know the only true God and the one whom he sent," the Truth. That is, only then do I in truth know the truth, when it becomes a life in me.[31]

For Anti-Climacus, any pursuit to know the truth without a greater pursuit to being the truth essentially entails untruth. Hence, the stress falls

30. CUP, 229–30.
31. PC, 206.

on "truthfulness" or "faithfulness" of the individual. As Pojman says, "'True' takes on its primitive meaning of 'faithful' ('troth'; in Danish, *Sandhed* has the same double meaning as our word 'truth')."[32] The proper order, which as an order of priority rather than chronology, is not from knowing to being but from being to knowing, because "knowing the truth is something which follows as a matter of course from being the truth." This "passion of the infinite is precisely subjectivity, and thus subjectivity is truth."[33] In that Pilate's question inversed this order to start with knowing (*the what*) without the primary concern for being (*the how*), it was trapped at an epistemological and semantic level and never traversed to the ontological and ethical levels. This, for Anti-Climacus, is untruth. Truth as subjectivity accentuates the relational dimension over against the propositional emphasis of the objective approach. The means to possess the truth is also the way to eternal life, which is to know relationally "the only true God and the one whom he sent."[34] This would mean that an existing individual possesses the truth by coming under the authority of Christ. Within existential thinking, an individual strives for truth that is actual and concrete because it affects his inmost being. The biblical assurance is that the knowledge of the truth sets one free.[35] A truth that frees the self is a truth that addresses the inner being. Accordingly, Climacus defines truth not as an idea but as a *relation* between the learner and the teacher, Christ, who himself is the Truth, both the medium and the message.

Notwithstanding the risk of oversimplification, it may be interesting to distinguish between the Old Testament Hebraic and later Greek approaches to life. The relative absence of abstraction in the Old Testament Hebrew usage and its prevalence in the Greek usage is noticeable. In the Old Testament Hebrew usage, instead of abstract words such as wisdom and goodness, these ideas are more often captured in instances, with particular references to a wise woman or a good man. "Knowledge" itself is not reduced to cognitive activity but is integrated into affective and practical living contexts.[36] A knowledgeable person then is not someone who

---

32. Pojman, *The Logic of Subjectivity*, 67. Pojman also has a good account of different approaches in connection to Kierkegaard and epistemology. See 63–75.

33. CUP, 203.

34. PC, 206. cf. John 17:3.

35. John 8:32.

36. When the Old Testament talks about Adam knowing Eve, it was more than a mental understanding. The phrase "he knew" is used to depict the greatest appropriation of love, consummated at the physical, emotional and spiritual levels of Adam's existence.

merely knows these ideas mentally, but who acts and lives wisely. Knowing in this sense is subjective because it involves the will and the very being of the subject. Greek philosophical thinking, on the other hand, elevated the universal categories above the particular practice and thus was inclined to capture an idea in its abstract form. However, along with this possibility also came the possibility of addressing abstract ideas devoid of a personal commitment. In the present milieu where the professor replaces the priest, the criteria for the position of, say, a professor of ethics are his ability to theorize and write books and not necessarily an ability to live according to certain ethical commitments. This method, epitomized in the Hegelian system, transformed the existing individual into a purely rational construction, thereby separating the moral from the rational.

In all this, it is important to remember that Climacus' purpose is not in any way to deny the existence of objective truth in the sense that there is a correct explanation of reality. Nor is his contention against a representational nature of truth, which, if it were the case, would also militate against any portrayal of what subjectivity would be. Rather, his contention is just that a systemic undertaking of the world-historical rightly belongs to God and not man. Keeping Hegel in mind, Climacus writes revealingly, "Is there then not such a system? That is not at all the case. Neither is this implied in what has been said. Existence itself is a system—for God, but it cannot be a system for any existing [*existerende*] spirit. System and conclusiveness correspond to each other, but existence is the very opposite. . . . Existence is the spacing that holds apart; the systematic is the conclusiveness that combines."[37]

In a sense, what Climacus labors to do is to move from the way of abstraction to a way of concrete thinking with no dichotomy between the propositional and personal, the rational and relational commitments. Truth has a definite function: to lead to a trusting submission, not just to a general submission to an idea but to a demand that is personalized for my life. Thus in his *Journals*, Kierkegaard reflects: "What matters is to find my purpose, to see what it really is that God wills that I shall do; the crucial thing is to find a truth that is truth for me, to find the idea for which I am willing to live and die. Of what use would it be to me to discover a so-called objective truth. . . . Of what use would it be to me for truth to stand before me, cold and naked, not caring whether or not I acknowledged it, making me uneasy

---

37. CUP, 118.

rather than trustingly receptive."[38] Thus, in a context where the objective pursuit of truth distanced from the self gave rise to a soulless Christianity, Kierkegaard raised an important question: how can an individual find the truth that is truth for him, for which he can live and die? This question then is central to subjectivity.

## Subjectivity and the Leap of Faith

Human self-deception "allows some time to elapse, an interim called: 'we shall look at it tomorrow.' During all this, knowing becomes more and more obscure, and the lower nature gains the upper hand..."[39] Contrary to such a deferral that rationalization brings about, subjectivity entails action, and not just any action but more precisely, a leap of faith. Christian beliefs are teleologically positioned as they are viewed and weighed from the vantage point of their purposiveness. The events in history are a fulfillment and hence fall in line with God's purposes. Otherwise, as J. H. Whittaker points out, there is no "saving virtue in holding an opinion about invisible, imperceptible objects in a transcendent order of reality.... The virtue which 'saves' is the virtue of conforming one's thoughts and practice to the distinctive perspective opened up by Christianity."[40] In other words, *metabasis eis allo genos*[41] [shifting from one genus to another] that Kierkegaard talks about is a transition, "Into teleological ways of thinking..., from ordinary thoughts to ultimate teleological judgments.... It consists of a genuine change in the *kinds* of judgments of history to the purposeful interpretations of faith. Supernatural entities are postulated simply because Christian judgments of purpose supervene, or supersede, all other purposeful considerations. Their supernatural form, I believe, is simply the sign of their supervenient role."[42]

In the preface to *Fear and Trembling*, Johannes de Silentio's primary target once again is Hegel. The references to "our age," or "our time" (in the preface) are directed to the prevailing philosophical climate about which the author is unhappy and he longs for the past to return when "faith was

---

38. JP, 5: 5100.
39. PC, 206.
40. Whittaker, "Kierkegaard on History and Faith," 387–88.
41. A phrase that both Lessing and Climacus borrow from Aristotle.
42. Whittaker, "Kierkegaard on History and Faith," 388.

a task for a whole lifetime."[43] Though Hegel's philosophy, which the author repeatedly refers to as "the system," has transposed "the whole content of faith into conceptual form, it does not follow that he has comprehended faith, comprehended how he entered into it or how it entered into him."[44] Essentially, such a systemization transforms the Christian faith (*pistis*) into knowledge (*gnosis*) or a Christian philosophical system. This exchange of true discipleship for philosophizing is a way of circumventing truthful being by turning Christianity into a system. While this was the charge against Hegel's philosophy, Kierkegaard would have found Bultmann, or Teilhard de Chardin, who in different ways did the same—turned the saving gospel into a religious system, guilty too. Nevertheless, such turning of Christian faith into "a very rationalistic, very logical, very coherent Christian apologetics have not calculated with the possibility that their very sharp, critical, and analytical logic can be turned around 180 degrees and used against the Christian faith."[45]

Yet, Kierkegaard does not deny the importance of reason or the role of human cognitive faculty, which are essential to recognize the paradox. Rather, he considers reason as being grossly inadequate to issue faith. However, while he does not deny the possibility of rational thinking occasioning a God-encounter leading to faith, he is weary and pessimistic about the use of the rational mode itself. He writes, "At its highest, inwardness in an existing subject is passion; truth as a paradox corresponds to passion, and that truth becomes a paradox is grounded precisely in its relation to an existing subject. In this way the one corresponds to the other."[46] After one's reason recognizes the intellectual absurdity of an article of faith, one affirms the incarnation of God, not by invoking certain cerebral criteria, but rather, as a "leap of faith."

The phrase "leap of faith," says Jamie Ferreira, "involves a circularity insofar as it seems to imply that the leap is made *by* faith."[47] That is, the leap *into* faith itself seems to be caused *by* faith. Though the phrase has come to be associated with Kierkegaard, he does not use any Danish equivalent of the phrase.[48] He does, however, refer to a qualitative transition to religious-

43. FT, 7.
44. FT, 7.
45. Ramm, *After Fundamentalism*, 67.
46. CUP, 199.
47. Ferreira, "Faith and the Kierkegaardian Leap," 207.
48. Ibid.

ness through concepts such as a leap (*spring*), transition (*Overgang*), qualitative (*qvalitativ*), and transition from one genus to another (*meta-basis eis allo genos*). Even the concept of a leap *to* faith, which is central to Kierkegaard's writings, cannot be obtained as a "theory of the leap" or "as a piece of information."[49] Yet it is evident in Kierkegaard's theory of stages that an individual who despairs within a vicious cycle or encounters a cul-de-sac within a sphere of existence—aesthetic, ethical, or religiousness A—has to make a leap to the religiousness B. The leap is also implied in an individual's response to what the absolute teacher, Christ, bestows as a gift, in that he lets go of all else that he previously held onto and his new anchor is God, which then is a leap of faith or a leap to faith.

## Self as a Becoming Self

One's personal development is ushered by a subjective appropriation of the knowledge the self already possesses. As Kierkegaard writes in his *Papers*, "The only fundamental basis for understanding is that one himself becomes what he understands and one understands only in proportion to becoming himself that which he understands."[50] In addition to the ontological nature of the self, Kierkegaard accentuates becoming as an ethical undertaking. For Climacus, "One who is existing is continually in the process of *becoming*; the actually existing subjective thinker, thinking, continually reproduces this in his existence and invests all his thinking in *becoming*."[51] In other words, rightly understood, the individual's existing is a becoming.[52] As Henriksen says, "Kierkegaard through his construction of the understanding of religion, makes the believing and existing subject a subject that is in becoming. Every becoming precludes the rational reconstruction of religion, since the content of religion cannot be adequately thought of independently of the subject (person) in question."[53]

A conception of the individual as *becoming* immediately replaces the security of fixity with instability or flux. A definite casualty in Climacus' view of the self is the feeling of certitude associated with fixity of the modern-Enlightenment framework. According to Climacus, "The perpetual

---

49. Ibid., 208.
50. JP, 2: 2299.
51. CUP, 86. (emphasized)
52. CUP, 196.
53. Henriksen, *The Reconstruction of Religion*, 107.

process of becoming is the uncertainty of earthly life, in which everything is uncertain."[54] He acknowledges that it is tempting to define existence as "something finished," because the reality of uncertainty "could bring a sensate person to despair, for one continually feels an urge to have something finished, but this urge is of evil and must be renounced."[55] Within a Climacean hermeneutic of finitude, a posture of being in control, with its characteristic arrogance, is evil primarily because it is, at its root, a denial of human contingency and finitude. Defining existence as something finished is a characteristic of the modern-Enlightenment arrogance with its declared autonomy that removes a dependence on God as the constituting other. A final definition of existence is impossible for the individual as he is a participant within existence. However, this urge for autonomy is characteristic not merely of the modern-Enlightenment but of every age. It is a repetition of the Adamic fall, which resulted from a desire for power based on the devil's promise that man would be like God if he ate of the forbidden fruit. Climacus' warning against the urge to define human existence as finished is in view of what such a definition would entail for the constituent structure of the self. Since a final definition belongs only to God, the author of existence, any defining of human existence as finished is a redoubling of the original Adamic act to take the place of God.

To decide for Christianity is to commit oneself to a pursuit of truth via subjectivity. While this entails a self-reflection, it is not an abstract contemplation of Christian doctrines, but a self-examining reflection by way of relating to the God who establishes the self. To reflect upon a relationship is to reflect upon the self. The focus of such a reflective self is not metaphysical but ethical, for the metaphysical does not even lend itself as a possible sphere of existence in Kierkegaardian calculus. For "the only reality there is for an existing person is his own ethical (reality); all other reality he only has knowledge about, but genuine knowledge is a translation into possibility."[56] Self-examination therefore is a way of life for the individual who exists in subjectivity.

In *Sickness Unto Death*, defining the self as a relational being, Anti-Climacus writes, "The self is a relation that relates itself to itself or is the relation's relating itself to itself in the relation; the self is not the relation but is the relation's relating itself to itself. . . . Such a relation that relates itself

---

54. CUP, 86.
55. CUP, 86.
56. Cited by Henriksen, *Reconstruction of Religion*, 113.

*Truthing through Subjectivity*

to itself, a self, must either have established itself or have been established by another. If the relation that relates itself to itself has been established by another, then the relation is indeed the third, but this relation, the third, is yet again a relation and relates itself to that which established the entire relation."[57] For Anti-Climacus, the self is not self-constituted, which entails two implications. First, the self owes its existence to an agent external to itself—God. Second, how the self should exist, "the ideal—the true self—is a self that conforms to the image of humanity revealed by God in the person of Christ,"[58] is also given externally. God as the constituting other does not come into the picture as an uninvolved agent in the deistic sense. Rather, God comes in as the co-participant other, who helps the self in its pursuit of authenticity. Thus, to be rooted in God is to be in the truth, and to be rooted in oneself (Socratic knower or Lessing's rational religion) is to be in untruth. The pursuit of an authentic self takes place by combining the two factors: a) by being rooted in God and b) by relating to oneself through self-examination.

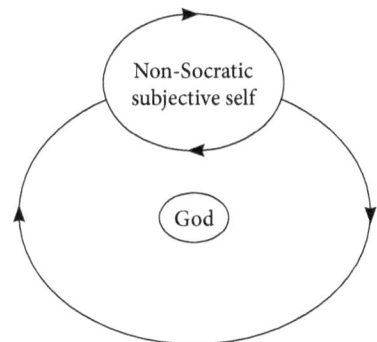

figure 01. The task of subjective development

The above diagram illustrates two dimensions of the self: a revolutionary cycle and a rotational cycle. The revolutionary cycle around God, who establishes the self, illustrates that God acts as the fulcrum that anchors the self, without whose power the self would be directionless and out of its orbit. The rotatory cycle enables the self to be self-reflective, which is an essential feature for an individual's growth. Thus, an individual is at the same time established from without by God and ethically self-examining from within. As Stephen Evans points out, Kierkegaard views the self as

57. SUD, 13.
58. Hannay, see introduction to SUD, 11.

both "ontological and ethical" where the self is seen "*both* as something I am *and* something I must become, *both* as a substance *and* as something to be achieved."[59] One errs in emphasizing any one aspect at the expense of the other. Only in relating to God does the individual get his identity, without which one would never know what to become. Further, it is not possible to be grounded in Christ without the subjective commitment to become authentic. In other words, standing before God and spiritual reflection brings about the maturity that takes into account one's social obligations. Just as human freedom is not a human product but granted by God, the exercise of human freedom within social relations requires divine recognition. Only in the obedience to the command to love can the otherwise inevitable reduction and objectification of humans as entities or units within a larger overarching scheme, be avoided.

Such a call of the ethical is compelling not in a generic spiritual sense, but in a distinctly Christian sense. Reflecting upon his own spiritual becoming, Kierkegaard wrote, "How imperfect I still am; and that I perhaps will get through life somehow, tested only in a mitigated kind of martyrdom, is evidence, of course, that I have not pursued it to perfection."[60] This task is possible only by recognizing the constituted and relational nature of the self, maintained by faith in God, which is "the opposite of being in despair."[61] His status as a becoming Christian is pictured in the following hypothetical situation. He writes, "With a sword hanging over my head, I am ordered to say whether or not I am a Christian. My answer would be: I trust to God that I am a Christian; I believe that out of grace he will accept me as a Christian."[62]

## Truthing Relation of the Self

### Self and the Absolute "Other"

It is sometimes assumed that Kierkegaard's thinking promotes a type of individualism, which lacks the emphasis on the relational nature of the self. However, as Westphal clarifies, "It is clearly not a Cartesian individualism, in either of the two possible senses of that phrase. For, on the one hand,

59. Evans, "Kierkegaard's View of the Unconscious," 83.
60. PV, 140.
61. SUD, 49.
62. PV, 135.

there is utterly nothing solipsistic about it. . . . On the other hand, there is nothing of that autonomy, that freedom from all authority . . ."[63] Rather, the type of individualism that emanates from Kierkegaard's thinking is better understood as *standing alone*. True to his project, *standing alone* ought to be judged for its enormous spiritual value. For it avoids the dangerous "herd sense"[64] and allows one to function as an individual even within a community. Given that one could err in moving towards the extremes of either an autonomous individualism or a stifling communalism, Kierkegaard's insights are indeed helpful to enable a *standing alone* and, at the same time, a *standing together*.

The Kierkegaardian notion of the self maintains an intrinsic worth of each individual better than a view that merely situates the self as an entity either within a socio-ethnic/communal paradigm or within the grand outworking of history. It is not just Hegelian thinking that sacrifices individuality at the altar of a larger overarching reality; the Marxian project, a child and critique of Hegelian philosophy, also sacrifices true individuality within its utopian egalitarianism. The contradiction of the Marxian system in defining emancipation compelled via egalitarianism is that it cannot be achieved unless individual voices that come against it are silenced, and thereby the individual, who should be emancipated, is counted as dispensable.

Not only does being related to Christ add value to life but also in that Christ is the prototype, he provides an image to imitate. What does it entail for an individual to be the truth? Becoming truthful is, therefore, a mimetic act where a follower imitates Christ who is the Truth. The imitation is fundamentally based in the recovery of *imago dei* in a disciple, an image, which "in him [Jesus Christ] the whole fullness of deity dwells bodily."[65] Christ the prototype provides "an example" for a disciple to "follow in his steps."[66] *Imitatio Christi*, therefore, is the process of truthing where truth takes its most authentic form, which is to be like Christ. Consequently, God as Truth is primarily understood as a *standing-under* (understanding) God in a personal relationship, and only secondarily understood through doctrines. The focus therefore is upon transforming the inner being rather than informing the mind. Thus Anti-Climacus writes, "No, the being of

---

63. Westphal, "Kierkegaard's Psychology and Unconscious Despair," 48.
64. TA, 62.
65. Col 2:9.
66. 1 Pet 2:21.

truth is the redoubling of truth within yourself, within me, within him, that your life, my life, his life expresses the truth approximately in the striving for it, that your life, my life, his life is approximately the being of the truth in the striving of it, just as the truth was in Christ a life, for he was the truth. And therefore, Christianly understood, truth is obviously not to know the truth but to be the truth."[67]

Anti-Climacean association of truth with being and not knowing is to be construed as a support for neither irrationalism nor a removal of Christian doctrine; rather, that truth understood as doctrines, acquires only a dependent significance in the context of subjectivity. In other words, Kierkegaard implies that an individual should, in all earnestness, seek to answer the "how" of life, and the "what" will be given. Lest we misunderstand that the propositional nature of truth is entirely lost in Kierkegaard, he clarifies in his *Journals*: "In all the usual talk that Johannes Climacus is mere subjectivity, etc., it has been completely overlooked that in addition to all his other concretions he points out in one of the last sections that the remarkable thing is that there is a How with the characteristic that when the How is scrupulously rendered the What is also given, that this is the How of 'faith.'"[68] Yet, shifting the essence of Christianity to a relationship rather than emphasizing a mental accent to certain doctrines, Kierkegaard sees a problem in pursuing rational proofs for the demonstration of Christianity. If faith essentially were a relation, passion would become its nature. As he writes, "when faith begins to lose passion, that is, when, faith begins to cease to be faith, then the demonstration is made necessary in order to enjoy general esteem from unbelief."[69] This implies that faith ceases to be faith in the absence of a relation with God and proofs are pursued to compensate for a lack of that relationship.

While it is the nature of the self to relate itself to itself, and to another, a self relates to God fundamentally as the power that establishes it. Thus, he writes, "The formula that describes the state of the self when despair is completely rooted out is this: in relating itself to itself and in willing to be itself, the self rests transparently in the power that established it."[70] Although the "other" in Kierkegaard does not always refer to God, the primacy given to God as the other over humans as the other, is pivotal. The God-

67. PC, 205.
68. JP, 4: 4550.
69. CUP, 30–31.
70. SUD, 14.

relation as the establishing power may appear metaphysical. However, for Kierkegaard, God is not a metaphysical entity but rather a relational being. The Kierkegaardian corrective to Hegel is to offer a God who is personal and not merely propositional, relational and not merely rational. D. Z. Phillips summarizes it well: "In the everyday grammar of religion, the relation between the believer and God is primary, and theological or philosophical attempts to take as foundational the project of 'proving God's existence' metaphysically tend to ignore actual religious practice. Kierkegaard's existential method at least has the merit of not ignoring practice."[71]

Despite an emphatic case for God as the other, argues Stephen Evans, it is strange that many scholars find Kierkegaard's view of the self relationally deficient. He records several cases as instances. John Elrod for instance, regrets that Kierkegaard seems to "pay no attention to the ontological and epistemological roles played by the other in the development of a concept of the self."[72] Similarly, Sylvia Walsh thinks that in the first part of *The Sickness Unto Death* there is an "absence of a relation to others in Kierkegaard's general description of the self," especially in view that Kierkegaard develops it in *Works of Love*.[73] To find Kierkegaard's view of the self as deficient, despite his repeated reference to the "other," argues Evans, "most obviously and most importantly . . . assume that God somehow doesn't count as a genuine 'other person.'"[74]

Similar to the accounts that fail to see God as a genuine "other" are also accounts that see God as just an instance of the other, thus relativizing the individual's relation to God. Derrida, for instance, sees God as merely an instance of the "other" in the story of Abraham's sacrifice of Isaac. He writes that it is "the paradox which inhabits the concept of duty or of absolute responsibility. This concept puts us into relation (without relation, and in the double secret) with the absolute other, with the absolute singularity of the other, of which God is here the name."[75] Likewise, Caputo suggests that "the name of God, of the biblical God of Abraham and Isaac, need not mean God for us. . . . God's mind is wholly other to Abraham, as is the mind

---

71. Phillips, *The Concept of Prayer*, 12.

72. Cited by Evans, "Kierkegaard's View of the Unconscious," 82. Cf. Elrod, "Kierkegaard on Self and Society."

73. Cited by Evans, "Kierkegaard's View of the Unconscious," 82. Cf. Sylvia Walsh, "On 'Feminine' and 'Masculine' Forms of Despair," 125.

74. Evans, "Kierkegaard's View of the Unconscious," 83.

75. Cited by Caputo, "Instants, Secrets, and Singularities," 222. Cf. Derrida, "*Donner la mort*," in *L'Ethique du don*, 66.

of every other, my friends and my family, who are as transcendent to me as Yahweh."⁷⁶ Furthermore, for Caputo, "responsibility is in the first place responsibility to the other, and the name of God is the name of the absolute other, so the story tells of my obligation, in my singularity, to the absolute singularity of the other."⁷⁷ That is "the otherness of God is paradigmatic of all otherness, of the otherness of all others."⁷⁸ Therefore, Abraham's sacrifice is seen as characteristic and paradigmatic of every human relationship. Thus, Caputo writes:

> The story of Abraham, this story of the absolute incommensurability of the individual with the general, Derrida thinks, makes a general point, one of use in any religion or outside religion, what Kierkegaard calls the "religious" is not confined to religion, and that is because it establishes the "logic" of absolute responsibility, which is the logic of a double bind. Whether one has faith or not, "there is a morality . . . in this story," the bind that descends upon every morality, the delimination or deconstruction of morality.⁷⁹

One has to differentiate between a postmodern view that sees the self as constituted by its relations to other selves, and a Kierkegaardian view of the self as constituted by the absolute "other"—God. While the former is a socio-ethical construct, the latter is an absolute relation in that God constitutes the self and provides the framework for the individual to relate socio-ethically with other selves. The absoluteness of relating to God as the absolute other is such that one has to love Isaac, Sarah and the entire ethical order, and yet sacrifice them. This God-relation makes the absolute demand, "If anyone comes to me and does not hate his own father and mother and wife and children and brothers and sisters, yes, and even his own life, he cannot be my disciple."⁸⁰ To transpose the self's nature of relationship with the absolute to any other self would be to miss the essential Kierkegaardian point, which is "to relate absolutely to the absolute *telos* and relatively to the relative ends."⁸¹ The priority given to God as the absolute other over the other human selves does not mean that one should fail to see every human other as "wholly other" in its singularity. This also does not

---

76. Caputo, "Instants, Secrets, and Singularities," 222.
77. Ibid., 223.
78. Ibid., 227.
79. Ibid. 222.
80. Luke 14:26.
81. CUP, 414.

mean that the other selves do not count in the final analysis, or that they are devoid of an intrinsic worth that is absolute.

Levinas gives a similar misreading of Kierkegaard's account of the Mount Moriah narrative. Levinas redefines what Kierkegaard understands as the teleological suspension of the ethical (the moral law against murder) in favor of the religious (obedience to sacrifice Isaac) in the Abrahamic story. With the turn of events where Abraham stops the sacrifice of Isaac and instead sacrifices a ram, Levinas sees a "return to the ethical, a teleological suspension of the religious, as it were in the name of the ethical."[82] However, the real point of the narrative is that Abraham's decision to sacrifice was an action that he had carried out prior to the actual doing of it. He had already sacrificed Isaac before he could kill him. Here, being ready to act is as good as the action itself. Therefore, it is not really a return to the ethical, for just as Abraham had received the command to sacrifice Isaac, he now receives the command not to kill his son, as the sacrifice had been already made. For Kierkegaard, God is not only a genuine other who constitutes the self and gives it an ideal for its becoming, but also, contra Derrida and Caputo, God is an absolute non-negotiable other, perhaps best represented with a capital O.

## Neighbor-Love and the Self

The command to love forms an important theme for Kierkegaard in his *Works of Love*. The pivotal aspect of truthing is *imitatio Christi*, where Christ the prototype becomes the model for a believer to imitate. Christian life therefore is a mimetic act that entails a resolution to imitate Christ, just as "the apostles, in conformity with their prototype, resolved to love, to suffer, to endure all things, to be sacrificed in order to save this unloving world."[83] Love as the highest virtue and as an act of discipleship takes the central place in the act of imitation.

Given the priority of God as the absolute Other, it is important to understand that the Kierkegaardian calculus automatically prioritizes between the first and the second command of Christ. The point in the biblical narrative is that it is the prioritizing of the God-ward love over neighbor-love that enables Abraham to listen to God's voice, which in that instance supersedes his love for Isaac, Sarah, and the moral order. The distinction in

82. Caputo, "Instants, Secrets, and Singularities," 226.
83. FSE, 85.

one's love for God and neighbor, though subtle, is important. While love for God demands all of one's heart, soul, mind, and strength, neighbor-love is patterned after self-love. The God-ward love that demands the whole individual is neither paradigmatic nor a prototype for neighbor-love. Whereas, human self-love serves as a prototype for neighbor-love as the command "contains what is presupposed, that every person loves himself."[84]

The prioritizing does not entail that the love for the neighbor suffers; rather, it audaciously presupposes that the only way that neighbor-love is best practiced is in prioritizing the absolute Other. It presupposes that the divine command would possess no practical authority without first prioritizing God-ward devotion. In this sense, the first command becomes a prerequisite for the second. Conversely, if neighbor-love were based on any human arbitration, it would essentially negate it, as it would lack a transcendental reference point.

A follower of Christ encounters love not as a concept but as a command. The question then is "can love be commanded?"[85] It would appear that an imperative or a command militates against the very nature of love, which should flow naturally rather than be compelled. However, the command to love can be understood in two ways. First, the command is precisely in the context of the human incapacity for it. If something were within natural capacity, a command would be superfluous. Thus, no command is required to practice romantic love or love for one's child as there seems to be a natural capacity for it. However, even those loves that are natural to begin with, become a lifelong commitment only in the context of neighbor-love. Thus, despite natural human capacity for romantic love, the necessity for neighbor-love within marriage mandates the command, "husbands love your wives,"[86] and needs to be understood as a requirement beyond romantic love. Second, the command is to be understood primarily in the context of the disciple's call to imitate Christ, the prototype. The new command to disciples is to love one another as Christ loved them—"A new command I give to you, that you love one another; even as I have loved you, that you also love one another."[87] Although the command to love already exists in Deut 6:4 and Lev 19:18, they are transformed into a new command

---

84. WL, 17.

85. I am indebted to a conversation with Myron B. Penner for this line of thinking.

86. Eph 5:25. The command is for husbands to love their wives as Christ loved the church. The command therein is to practice *agape* love.

87. John 13:34.

by Christ who presents himself as a prototype for the disciples. Thus, the followers of Christ are called to a higher benchmark in their practice of love in that they have the highest pattern to imitate. The purview of this "inter-disciples" love, although to be practiced among them, is not meant to be restrictive within the church. Thus, the new commandment, "Greater love has no one than this, that a man lay down his life for his friends,"[88] is a mimetic repetition of Christ's love that led him to lay his life for his disciples, whom he called "friends."

The ontological priority of God over humans places the command to love the Lord as necessarily prior to the command to love one's neighbor. Furthermore, it should not be assumed that one's neighbor-love conflicts or competes with one's love for God. Rather, the love for God complements neighbor-love and makes it possible.[89] For Kierkegaard, neighbor-love is ultimately rooted in the redemptive love of God for humanity and emanates from God himself. In the section on "Love's Hidden Life" in his *Works of Love*, Kierkegaard writes, "Just as the quiet lake originates deep down in hidden springs no eye has seen, so also does a person's love originate even more deeply in God's love. If there were no gushing spring at the bottom, if God were not love, then there would be neither the little lake nor a human being's love. Just as the quiet lake originates darkly in the deep spring, so a human being's love originates mysteriously in God's love."[90]

Conversely, what really competes with love for God is self-love! Kierkegaard also understands that a proper self-love is a prerequisite for a proper neighbor-love. Thus, he writes, "Therefore if anyone is unwilling to learn from Christianity to love himself in the right way, he cannot love the neighbor either. . . . To love yourself in the right way and to love the neighbor correspond perfectly to one another."[91] Yet, understandably, one sees no explicit command to self-love as it is taken for granted. An improper self-love would then compete with one's love for God and one's neighbor-love. Thus, it is pivotal that one knows that it is "possible for anyone to misunderstand this, as if it were Christianity's intention to proclaim self-love as a

---

88. John 15:13.

89. "If anyone says, 'I love God,' and hates his brother, he is a liar; for he who does not love his brother whom he has seen, cannot love God whom he has not seen." 1 John 4:20–21.

90. WL, 9–10.

91. WL, 22.

prescriptive right? Indeed, on the contrary, it is Christianity's intention to wrest self-love away from us human beings."[92]

## Conclusion

Kierkegaard's argument is not just that truth is elusive in an objective sense, but that it is quite comical to romanticize objective truth-pursuits with decidedly no self-concern. Consequently, Kierkegaard argues that Truth is Subjectivity. Just as truth is availed at the moment of incarnation, subjectivity is the human response to the Christ, the truth that is revealed. One thus becomes subjective to the extent of relating to the God who establishes the individual in trust and passion.

It is possible that one misunderstands Kierkegaard's focus on subjectivity as implying a type of subjectivism or arbitrariness. In the next chapter, I shall consider Climacus' parable of the penitent idolater to engage an important Climacean question. Climacus asks, "Where there is more truth . . . whether on the side of the person who only objectively seeks the true God and the approximating truth of the God-idea or on the side of the person who is infinitely concerned that he in truth relate himself to God with the infinite passion of need. . . . Where, then, is there more truth?"[93]

---

92. WL, 17.
93. CUP, 201.

# 3

# Being in the Truth:
# Re-Engaging Climacus' Devout Idolater

*If someone who lives in the midst of Christianity enters, with knowledge of the true idea of God, the house of god, the house of the true God, and prays, but prays in untruth, and if someone lives in an idolatrous land but prays with all the passion of infinity, although his eyes are resting upon the image of an idol— where, then, is there more truth?* — CUP, 201.

IN HIS FAMOUS PARABLE of the devout idolater, Kierkegaard's pseudonym Johannes Climacus poses the following question:

> Now, if the problem is to calculate where there is more truth . . . whether on the side of the person who only objectively seeks the true God and the approximating truth of the God-idea or on the side of the person who is infinitely concerned that he in truth relate himself to God with the infinite passion of need—then there can be no doubt about the answer for anyone who is not totally botched by scholarship and science. *If someone who lives in the midst of Christianity enters, with knowledge of the true idea of God, the house of god, the house of the true God, and prays, but prays in untruth, and if someone lives in an idolatrous land but prays with all the passion of infinity, although his eyes are resting upon the image of an idol—where, then, is there more truth? The one prays in truth*

> to God although he is worshipping an idol; the other prays in un-
> truth to the true God and is therefore in truth worshipping an idol.[1]

Where, then, is there more truth? As Westphal observes, "The question is not where the objective truth is to be found. That is stipulated in a way that Climacus expects his readers to share."[2] Instead, the question relates solely to the subjective appropriation of that truth, and in that respect the parable places the idolater far above the one who is praying to the (objectively) true God but in (subjective) untruth. The idolater, who is worshipping an idol, nevertheless "prays in truth to God."

The phrases "more truth" and "worshipping an idol" immediately raise the question of the truth relations among various religions. That the books Kierkegaard writes under his own name seldom treat such a topic is hardly surprising, in view of the fact that he is writing for Danes, for whom conversion to some other world religion is not an immediate prospect. If he had been writing to non-Christians, for example, he might have had to approach things in quite another way. Thus, in a draft for the unpublished essay "Armed Neutrality," he writes, "If my relation were to pagans, I could not be neutral; then in opposition to them I would have to say that I am a Christian."[3]

Within Kierkegaard's pseudonymous authorship, on the other hand, such a topic fits very well, and the pseudonymous author, Johannes Climacus, who writes the above parable, is just the right person for the task. Challenging, speculative thought-experiments are Climacus' specialty. Indeed, if Climacus' own account of how he came to write *Postscript* is to be trusted, his involvement with writing that whole book arose merely because, while every other pastime he could imagine seemed too boring, this one "appealed to" him "like a complicated criminal case."[4] In the spirit of Climacus, then, I propose the following new thought-experiment, in order to identify a possible "subjective" context for Climacus' concept of the devout idolater.

---

1. CUP, 201. Italics added. This parable is a distant echo of Jesus' statement in Matt 8:10–13: "'Truly, I say to you, not even in Israel have I found such faith. I tell you, many will come from east and west and sit at table with Abraham, Isaac, and Jacob in the kingdom of heaven, while the sons of the kingdom will be thrown into the outer darkness; there men will weep and gnash their teeth.' And to the centurion Jesus said, 'Go; be it done for you as you have believed.'"

2. Westphal, "Climacus on Subjectivity and the System," 141.

3. PV, 138–39.

4. CUP, 241.

## A Project of Thought—Locating the Devout Idolater

What kind of subjective faith might one attribute to Climacus' "devout idolater"? The first issue to deal with, surely, is what the object of faith for such a believer might be. The idolater's prayer, for example, seems to indicate a genuine ignorance of Christian revelation. It is thereby unlikely to qualify as an instance of Christian faith according to the Climacean schema, since it lacks the essential "mark of standing in relation to the god's having come into existence."[5] For Climacus, Christian faith, properly speaking, includes faith in the incarnation of Christ. Otherwise, Climacus says almost nothing here about what the content of the devout unbeliever's faith *is*; he indicates only what it is *not*.

Still, the parable does supply one clue. A reader cannot help noticing that the parable locates this idolater, not in Denmark or in some other predominantly Christian country, but "in an idolatrous land." The geographical distancing of the idolater from the Christian world possibly suggests that he has never heard of Christ. Whether an idolater living in Denmark would attract much sympathy from Climacus is doubtful in any case, since the person who encounters preaching about Christ and yet remains an idolater would, in Climacus's view, be coming before the idol not in self-annihilation but in self-assertiveness; offense would arise, rather than faith. Ideally, one has no reason to remain an idolater where the true God is revealed.

Where, then, might one find the devout idolater? Just before that question is answered, it may be clarified that Climacus finds that the worshipper of the true God is just as accidentally situated in a "Christian" land as the idol worshipper is placed in an idolatrous land. Lessing's "ugly ditch" or the problem of the historical gap between the present and the first century has a parallel in the geographical distance between one who lived in early Palestine and another who lives in a distant idolatrous land. However, Climacus' argument is that being situated in the Christian world is just a quantitative approximation and is of no particular advantage for coming to faith. Geographical proximity, just as historical proximity, in itself is not a vehicle of religious truth and is therefore insignificant.

But given that the new thought-project requires some specific cultural context, why not locate the devout idolater in India? With its hundreds of millions of people, India is more likely to offer remote villages where Jesus is unknown than many other nations. Moreover, in India there is

---

5. CUP, 210.

an old, non-Christian tradition that displays some striking similarities to Christian faith, on its subjective side, and that is the *Viśiṣṭādvaitic* tradition propounded by the south Indian sage Rāmānuja. Therefore, let this thought-project locate Climacus' devout idolater within Rāmānuja's tradition, with its several recommended ways to salvation.

For Rāmānuja himself, the first two ways are themselves steps along the way that he expects his readers to follow, in order to arrive at the third. The first way is called *karma mārga*, or the way of action. Like the Mosaic Law, taken in a literal sense, the Hindu *karma mārga* is a way to salvation through works. In fact, like that Law, as found in the Hebrew Bible, the *karma mārga* also contains a large number of ritual prescriptions, along with its universal ethical injunctions. On the other hand, the *jñānā mārga*,[6] or way of knowledge, leads to salvation via knowledge and contemplation. Echoing the Socratic take on knowing, it recognizes "the human self as a center of knowing by the exercise of that very knowing itself and by developing that potency to its fullness of actualization through the knowing of God."[7] Like Socrates, the *jñānā yogin* defines sin essentially as ignorance. In Rāmānuja's day this way was powerfully represented by the tradition of *Advaita Vedānta*, which had drawn from the Upanishadic traditions the elements for a profound metaphysical system of absolute monism. The third way is called the *bhakti mārga*, or the way of devotion, and for Rāmānuja this is the highest way. The essence of *bhakti* comprises three factors: the direct experience of God (*anubhava*), the love generated by that experience (*prīti*), and the willful self-surrender resulting in human service (*kainkarya*). Like the *Advaita Vedānta* school, Rāmānuja also builds from the Upanishads at the same time as he disagrees with that school on many points. Rāmānuja argues that, where duality is completely excluded by a monism, there can be no place for the individual and for the individual's *bhakti* (love or devotion) toward the lord. By citing the *Mundaka Upanishad* 3.2.3 about the lord's relation to the believer, for example, Rāmānuja illustrates how some of the Upanishads can lead away from a monistic, to a pluralistic, reading.[8] Moreover, in his commentary on *Gītā* 2.29, Rāmānuja helps to undermine the class and gender divisions that the usual practice of *Advaita Vedānta* tended to reinforce.

6. See *Gītā*, Chapters 2, 4, 5, 6, and 13.

7. Raghavachar, "The Spiritual Vision of Rāmānuja," 266.

8. Cited by Lipner, *The Face of Truth*, 112. Cf. *The Vedānta-Sūtras with the Commentary of Rāmānuja*, Vol. 3, 284.

*Being in the Truth: Re-Engaging Climacus' Devout Idolater*

As the *Viśiṣṭādvaitic* traditions later developed, they placed more and more emphasis upon the independence and importance of what amounted to a fourth way to salvation, emphasizing *prapatti,* or surrender. A problem with the usual way of *bhakti* is that it is essentially the practice of a required discipline of established means (*sādhana*)[9] that has to be mastered in order for the seeker to attain salvation. Because it entails rigorous effort to master *bhakti* devotional practices, the way of *bhakti*, like that of *jñānā*, imposes a difficult, if not impossible, task upon virtually all seekers. From the standpoint of *prapatti,* both *jñānā* and bhakti ways are mere elaborations of the way of *karma*.

By centering on *prapatti,* on the other hand, a seeker without exceptional capacities can simply transfer the weight of one's burden to god (*bhara-samarpana*),[10] and thereby seek refuge under god's feet (*saranagati*).[11] In the words of a later leader within the *Viśiṣṭādvaitic* tradition, the prayer of the penitent might be: "Lord, I, who am nothing, conform to your will and desist being contrary to it, and with faith and prayer, submit to you the burden of saving my soul."[12] Such a prayer is a total submission of the will, intellect, and body to the mercy of god. A Christian reader can hardly help but recall the contrast that Jesus drew between the prayer of the Pharisee and that of the tax collector: "the tax collector, standing far off, would not even lift up his eyes to heaven, but beat his breast, saying, 'God, be merciful to me a sinner!'"[13]

With this last concept, *prapatti,* the new "project of thought" finally finds a fitting candidate for the role played by the devout idolater in Climacus' parable, that is, the role of someone fully realizing one's own nothingness, in truth and utter devotion. Whether this devout idolater, like the tax collector in the following verse of Luke's Gospel, "went down to his house justified," however, Climacus' parable does not say.

---

9. Disciplined effort or practice.

10. Submission of weight or burden.

11. The word literally means "to prostrate."

12. Vedanta Deśika, second stanza of "Nyāsadaśaka" (poem), cited in Raghavachar, "Spiritual Vision," 271. It reads, *Nyasyāmi akincanah śrīmannanukūlo hyavarjitah viśvāsa-prārthanā-pūrvam ātmaraksābharam tvayi.*

13. Luke 18:13. cf. Kierkegaard's "[The Tax Collector] Luke 18:13," in "Three Discourses at the Communion on Fridays," WA, 130–31.

# Truth and Subjectivity, Faith and History

## Climacean Considerations

The reader who already has some familiarity with the two books Kierkegaard published under the name "Johannes Climacus" will have noticed a strong similarity (and also some key differences) between the "project of thought" Climacus puts forward in his *Philosophical Fragments* and the new "project of thought" proposed here. The right way to proceed, therefore, may be to trace these parallels through those two texts, beginning with *Philosophical Fragments* and then proceeding to its massive *Postscript*.

The first chapter of *Philosophical Fragments* is a "project of thought" that defines the question for the book, by contrasting two hypotheses about how truth (at least, religious and philosophical truth) can be learned. According to hypothesis A, all a person can learn is what one already implicitly "knows"; that is to say, the philosopher can only analyze concepts that people share. According to hypothesis B, on the other hand, there might be a teacher whose teaching would so transform the pupils that they would acquire a new set of conceptual capacities and would be, in fact, new persons.[14] Socrates best represents the kind of teacher needed for the first hypothesis, and (without initially using Christ's name) Climacus implicitly postulates Christ as the teacher for the second. Once Christ has given the teaching, however, the Socratic Method becomes necessary for the second hypothesis as well, since the learners must now continually "recollect" what the divine teacher has taught.[15]

Climacus compares these two potential teachers with care. According to Socrates' method, he writes, truth is located within the individual, so that the responsibility of "recollecting" what is already known also lies within the individual.[16] Such teaching would, in fact, function as a process of self-actualization. With the divine teacher, on the other hand, the individual

---

14. PF, 18.

15. PF, 65.

16. PF, 9. Here Climacus refers to several of the Platonic dialogues, including the *Meno*, a central source for Plato's theory of recollection. Parallel to *Meno*'s Socratic idea of the immortal soul is the Hindu idea of re-incarnation of souls, which implies a soul that "has seen all things both here and in the other world, has learned everything that is. So we need not be surprised if it can recall the knowledge of virtue or anything else which, as we see, it once possessed. All nature is akin, and the soul has learned everything, so that when a man has recalled a single piece of knowledge—*learned* it, in ordinary language—there is no reason why he should not find out all the rest, if he keeps a stout heart and does not grow weary of the search, for seeking and learning are in fact nothing but recollection" (*Meno* 81 cd).

who is not in possession of the truth that God provides has no access to it whatsoever. God, the absolute teacher, gives both the truth and the condition for truth. In fact, in this hypothesis, the teacher *is* the teaching, so that to retain the "teaching," the learner must maintain a personal relationship with the teacher. For Climacus, that difference is decisive. The historical has to be part of Christian faith.

*Concluding Unscientific Postscript* is a very different book from *Philosophical Fragments*. Whereas the "project of thought" in *Fragments* is a good place to introduce what kind of a thinker Climacus is, its *Postscript* is where the "devout idolater," with total trust and surrender, can play a special role. The two books differ in how they treat the "how" and the "what" of the *Fragments*' project. While *Philosophical Fragments* deals primarily with "what" the divine teacher teaches, its postscript focuses on "how" the learner is to relate to that teaching. The "what" is the objective content, often called "objectivity"; while the "how" is the "subjectivity," which is the subject's appropriation of that content,

*Postscript* consists of two parts. In the first, Climacus mounts arguments against philosophers who, in their efforts to develop a comprehensive metaphysical system, play down, or even deny, the importance of individual existence. The second part devotes most of its pages to laying out three major aspects within the kind of religious subjectivity that he calls "religiousness A": resignation, suffering of conscience, and total guilt. Although Climacus introduces religiousness A as part of his analysis of Christian subjectivity, it would be easy to imagine someone pursuing the way of *prapatti* reading these pages and indeed resonating with *Postscript*'s call for a rigorous spiritual life. Finally, Climacus includes a few pages in which he outlines another kind of subjectivity, which he calls "religiousness B," that is, Christianity. As with the second, "B," hypothesis in *Philosophical Fragments*, this "B" option also requires a teaching (that is, a revelation) from the divine teacher, Christ. In *Postscript*, however, the emphasis is on "how" the learner appropriates that teaching rather than on "what" the teaching itself is.

Climacus' purpose in juxtaposing the two worshippers in the parable is not to argue toward a religious pluralism of any kind, but rather it is to argue for the worthlessness or even the depravity of believing in the true God, accompanied by an absence of true devotion. This juxtaposition hardly exhausts the array of possibilities wherein worshippers exist. Thus, one may infer four possibilities:

a. The true God is worshipped in truth.
b. An idol is worshipped in truth.
c. An idol is prayed to in untruth.
d. The true God is prayed to in untruth.

Climacus draws a contrast between b. and d. Yet it is reasonable to imply a. and c. as definite possibilities within the Climacean calculus. While a. and b. are cases of sincere devotion to an object of worship, c. and d. are cases of hypocritical responses. Yet, a. stands distinctly apart as a possibility only after the moment of faith, where truth and the condition for truth are given by the divine teacher. Since d. is the real target of Climacus, it becomes the worst case precisely on account of it lacking a subjectivity that should accompany the moment of faith and the condition. Climacus seems to affirm that more is expected from the one to whom more is revealed, in line with the New Testament passage, "For it would have been better for them never to have known the way of righteousness than after knowing it to turn back from the holy commandment delivered to them."[17]

However, one ought to avoid at all cost, a common misunderstanding of this passage in the *Postscript*, since Climacus seems to come across as ascribing greater subjectivity to mere truthful worship, while objectivity is assigned only a dependent or secondary merit. Although it is tempting to suppose that one could place religiousness A and religiousness B (Christianity) on the same "scale" of subjectivity, so that B was somewhere higher up the scale than A, that plan does not fit Climacus' overall account. Climacus understands religiousness B to be a *new* kind of subjectivity, one that is being continuously transformed by an encounter with Christ.[18] Thus, even though Climacus sometimes suggests that the subjectivity of religiousness B is "more passionate" than religiousness A, those statements could be misleading if they were taken out of context.[19] Since religiousness B's "passion" is qualitatively different from that of religiousness A, B cannot have "more" of the same passion than A. Christianity has a distinctive passion,

---

17. 2 Pet 2:21. Again, "Let not many of you become teachers, my brethren, for you know that we who teach shall be judged with greater strictness" (Jas 3:1).

18. CUP, 581–86.

19. In his notebooks at about the time of writing *Fragments*, Kierkegaard makes clear that there are different *kinds* of passions: "Let no one misinterpret all my talk about pathos [*Pathos*] and passion [*Lidenskab*] to mean that I intend to sanction every uncircumcised immediacy, every unshaven passion." JP, 3: 3127.

or subjectivity, of its own. In his notebooks Kierkegaard himself analyzes *Postscript* along those lines:

> In all this talk that Johannes Climacus is mere subjectivity, etc., it has been completely overlooked that in addition to all the other concretions he points out in one of his last sections[20] that the remarkable thing is that there is a How with the characteristic that when the How is scrupulously rendered the What is also given, that this is the How of "faith." Right here, at its very maximum, inwardness is shown to be objectivity. And this, then, is a turning of the subjectivity-principle which, as far as I know, has never before been carried through or accomplished in this way.[21]

That is to say: according to Climacus, Christianity has not only a distinctive, historically defined "what" but also an equally distinctive, historically conditioned "how."

## Kierkegaard, Climacus, the Devout Idolater, and Rāmānuja

In order to understand Climacus' parable in relationship to Rāmānuja, a reader has to bring in Kierkegaard too. There is no way to get around that, because Climacus is not in a position to tell the whole story. Climacus insists he "does not even pretend to be a Christian."[22] He only proposes to clarify Christian categories so that they will not be misused. The concept of the devout idolater cannot stand by itself, but eventually a reader has to put the issue into Kierkegaard's own context.

It is important to remember that the parable of the devout idolater is told to Christians, or, at least, to those who claim to be Christians even though they have lost their passion and dedication. Such Christians need to hear the parable in order to inspire them to take their beliefs more earnestly, because they are living under the illusion that they are somehow superior to the devout idolater, even though they are not. On the other hand, there would be no point in telling the parable to the devout idolater or to the penitent tax collector. Both of them are too busy prostrating themselves and contemplating their own unworthiness to have any desire to hear a report on how proficiently they are worshipping.

---

20. CUP, 612–13.
21. JP, 4: 4550.
22. CUP, 424.

From the perspective of an interested outside observer, such as Climacus, the situation looks different from the way it does to either kind of participant. Climacus would notice right away how well the faith of the devout idolater would fit into the category of general religiosity, religiousness A, which does not specify what the specific object of the worship may be. Moreover, even though they are distinguishable subjectivities, that is, different passions, Climacus would perceive that the practice of *prapatti* and the practice of Christianity (religiousness B) sometimes display some surprising similarities; for example in the kinds of prayers that might be offered. Who would be surprised, after all, if a devout Christian worshiper, not just in India, but in any part of the world, were to invoke God with the words: "Lord, I, who am nothing, conform to your will . . ."?

What, then, is the case of someone like Kierkegaard himself, who is both observer and participant? How would he see the person who is outside of Christianity, either the observer from outside Christianity, or the participant? The answer with respect to the interested observer from outside Christianity is obvious, because Kierkegaard continually dwells upon such a figure in his writings. That person is Socrates, a figure that occupied Kierkegaard's mind all the way from his dissertation to the very end of his life. Socrates represents the situation of the person who is not in a position to learn even the minimum about the divine teacher's message, such as the devout idolater. Socrates lived before Christ and could therefore not have known anything historical about him. The immense deference Climacus pays to Socrates and his method illustrates the depth of respect Kierkegaard himself has for Socrates, and also for all such intellectual figures as Lessing,[23] who stand outside or on the boundaries of Christian tradition.

On the basis of how Kierkegaard treats Socrates, one can be confident that he would feel the same kind of respect for such a figure as Rāmānuja too. Long before Climacus raised objections against the Hegelian philosophers' efforts to develop a comprehensive metaphysical system that would play down, or even deny, the importance of individual existence, Rāmānuja had already championed much the same kind of cause.[24] In several other respects, such as his egalitarianism, Rāmānuja was a Climacus figure before Kierkegaard.[25] Granted, there are important philosophical and theological disagreements between Kierkegaard and Rāmānuja; but, if one may judge

---

23. See "An Expression of Gratitude to Lessing," in CUP, 63–71.
24. CUP, 249. Agera, *Faith, Prayer and Grace*, 8.
25. CUP, 160, 227–228.

by how Kierkegaard treats Socrates[26] and Lessing[27] in *Postscript*, Kierkegaard would have been delighted to ignore any such differences and to edit his account of Rāmānuja to bring it as close to his own views as possible, especially if that suited his polemical purposes in some argument. From Kierkegaard's perspective, that Rāmānuja was not a Christian would only have made him a more positive figure to use as a model for philosophical method.

## Conclusion

How, then, might Kierkegaard himself (as opposed to Climacus) have judged the situation of the devout idolater, or of Rāmānuja, if he had discussed them within writings under his own name? Although this is a difficult, probably unanswerable question, it is possible to speculate what he might be willing to say.

For one thing, it is clear that Kierkegaard cared deeply about all the people he knew, without exception. Just before he died in 1855, Kierkegaard was involved in a fierce battle with the Danish State church. If Kierkegaard was right in attacking the church authorities, the argument of Climacus' parable would have left them in a much worse religious situation than either figure in the parable, because the authorities were in effect deliberately worshipping a false god (Mammon). Still, Kierkegaard rejected using such a Climacean calculus for judging others. Instead he drew upon his own experience of inexplicable grace. He recalled a remark by the late Bishop Mynster, who had said to him once that Kierkegaard seemed to think that all the others were condemned to hell. "No," Kierkegaard reflects, "if I can be said to speak at all of going to hell then I say something like this: If the others are going to hell, then I am going along with them. But I do not believe that; on the contrary, I believe that we will all be saved, I, too, and this awakens my deepest wonder."[28]

This belief, however, did not mean that he was prepared to make any dogmatic judgment in this regard. In *Upbuilding Discourses in Various Spirits* and *Works of Love*, for example, Kierkegaard interpreted human

---

26. Steffes, "Kierkegaard's Germanophone Socrates Sources," 305–306.

27. Stott, *Behind the Mask*, 96–98.

28. JP, 6: 6947. cf. JP, 6: 6934. Cited by Gouwens, "Kierkegaard on the Universally Religious and the Specifically Christian," 96, note 15. Gouwens also refers to other discussions of this remark by Gregor Malantschuk and Gordon Marino.

differences through a distinctively Christian concept of divine love. Invidious comparisons between people about dress or social ranks, for example, are inconsistent with the indiscriminate divine love with which all people have been showered, he wrote.[29] No human calculus can define who ranks higher or lower before God.[30] Thus the only appropriate human response to God's free grace is surprise and gratitude, coupled with an eagerness to share that love with everyone else. By Easter time the following year, Kierkegaard's convictions on this topic deepened, when he was personally overwhelmed by that kind of love, and the experience led him to a growing confidence that God had not only forgiven but forgotten all his sins.[31]

Accordingly, what Kierkegaard would *not* do with the devout idolater or Rāmānuja would be, from an observer's perspective, to announce that either of them was more or less likely to go to heaven or hell than anyone else. In fact, Kierkegaard would not do that for any other person either, since on such a personal matter he could only be an involved participant. God is the only one who could be an impartial observer in such a case. As the principle that echoes through C. S. Lewis' Narnia tale *The Horse and His Boy* says: God only tells you your own story.[32] While Kierkegaard could be blunt in his public denunciations of the hypocrisy and self-serving misrepresentations of Christianity by ecclesiastical authorities in Denmark, even in that case, regarding figures he knew personally, he left the judgment on their eternal destination up to God.

---

29. "What We Learn from the Lilies of the Field and the Birds of the Air," UDVS, 166–71; WL, 179–87. cf. Ferreira, "The Next Thing," 389–96.

30. Mark 10:40; Matt 20:23.

31. JP, 5: 6131. cf. JP, 5: 6135.

32. Chapters 11 and 14.

# PART II

History and Faith

# 4

## Understanding Historical Religious Knowledge for Faith

*Knowing a historical fact—indeed, knowing all the historical facts with the trustworthiness of an eyewitness—by no means makes the eyewitness a follower, which is understandable, because such knowledge means nothing more to him than the historical. — PF, 59.*

RELIGIOUS BELIEFS DO NOT necessarily have historical content. Where religious faith has historical content, it brings with it some problems associated with history. Conversely, where a religious faith is not connected to history, it remains isolated from the problems related to history. If historical content is imposed on a religious faith without it, either for want of greater authentication or for some other reason, it amounts to a confounding of facts and myths. This has been specifically noted in reference to the assertions made in the last two decades that have tried to mark Ayodhya, a North Indian town, as the exact birthplace of Lord Ram.[1] The inaptness of such an imposition of particular historical detail, to a narrative that is primarily mythical, is evident. While the absence of historical content enables a religious belief to avoid problems pertaining to historical religious

---

1. Amartya Sen, in his inaugural address to the 61st annual session of the Indian History Congress, reiterated this point, in reference to Ayodhya being the birthplace of Lord Ram. See Sen, "History and the Enterprise of Knowledge," 12.

knowledge, it also eliminates the possibility of corroborating a believer's faith or the possibility of knowing that one believes something real rather than something imagined. Hence, apart from the right-wing political motivations of such a reinterpretation, this could be indicative of the internal dilemma embedded in the ahistorical nature of the Hindu faith.

Similar to the confounding of the categories implicit in the historicizing of a mythological belief, is the problem of mythologizing of a historical religious belief. A case in point is the eighteenth- and nineteenth-century theological liberalism, which moved the central Christian idea of historical incarnation to the periphery of Christian faith and, in some cases, to a total dismissal of it. As inheritors of the liberal theological tradition, a thinking that reinterprets incarnation within the category of myth persists even today.[2] Such a confounding of the categories of myth and history does disservice to both historical and ahistorical religious traditions, by violating their essential character.

Consequently, Christ is regarded as a teacher of some noble truths, along with other religious leaders who have endeavored to dispense what they have come to understand as divine truths. The problem with theological liberalism is that the teacher becomes less important than his teaching, as in the case of other religions, where moral principles are emphasized rather than the historical presence of the eternal. Kierkegaard sees this as a reversal to a Socratic way of thinking, where the teacher is merely incidental. Thus in *Practice in Christianity,* Anti-Climacus laments, "Christ has been abolished altogether, thrown out and his teaching taken over, and finally he is almost regarded as one regards an anonymous writer: the teaching is the principal thing, is everything."[3]

## Modern Enlightenment and History: Positivist and Idealist Views

Following the French philosopher Auguste Comte (1798–1857), the positivist view undertook the study of history as a scientific project based on causal relations, which unearthed historical facts as disinterested observers. This view assumed "that historians would in due course uncover the 'laws' of historical development."[4] This objective view of history placed lesser

---

2. See John Hick's *The Myth of God Incarnate.*
3. PC, 123.
4. Tosh, *The Pursuit of History,* 109.

value on the historian's intuitions and personal judgments. "The legacy of positivism to modern historiography," according to Collingwood, led to the historian's "unprecedented mastery over small-scale problems with unprecedented weakness in dealing with large-scale problems."[5]

The modern-Enlightenment approach to history offered optimism in recovering and knowing what happened in the past. This optimism was furthered by scientific discoveries, which made explicit possibilities previously thought impossible. As Collingwood says, "The methods of modern historical inquiry have grown up under the shadow of their elder sister, the method of natural science."[6] Propelled by its new-found optimism, Enlightenment thinking sought to systematize methods of writing history by challenging those that existed. The purpose was to arrive at scientific certainty in historical analysis. Though no one succeeded in propounding a conclusive method or definition for the writing of history, it challenged several existing notions.

The most important notion that it challenged was that history was written to justify causes.[7] The reliability of a historical record was questioned if it was written to justify a particular cause. Thus, the Enlightenment approach to history sought to establish objectivity in historical inquiry, which guaranteed that no personal or biased interpretation crept into its writing. Historians worked towards arriving at a historical knowledge that was certain and final by an objective and unbiased examination of facts. This scientific history was supposed to be above the reproaches of any partisan affinity to any given cause. As a result of this, the science of archives came into being in the nineteenth century. The quest for unbiased scientific history required the careful scrutiny of documents, even those not intended for history, such as diaries, letters and ledgers, which would unravel the intentions behind the otherwise lifeless data. Viewed in this way the Gospel writers would, without a doubt, score poorly, when they claim to have written their account in order that their readers "may believe that Jesus is the Christ, the Son of God."[8]

The positivist position, in presupposing that historical processes were natural processes, considered history to be governed by natural laws. This entailed that just as natural laws could be discovered, so also history and

---

5. Collingwood, *The Idea of History*, 131–32.
6. Ibid., 228.
7. Ramm, *After Fundamentalism*, 72.
8. John 20:31.

the laws that governed the historical process could be discovered. Among the earliest thinkers to protest against the positivist view of history was R. G. Collingwood (1889–1943), who denounces the view that history was a "story of successive events." He writes, "The very meaning of the word has become debauched through the assimilation of historical process to natural process. Against misunderstandings arising from this source I am bound to protest, even if I protest in vain."[9] The problem with the positivistic approaches, including those pertaining to historical inquiry, is not just the unfounded optimism they created, but something more inherent to what they presupposed. Collingwood writes that the problem of the modernist approach to history was the "positivistic conception, or rather misconception, of history, as a study of successive events lying in a dead past, events to be understood as the scientist understands natural events, by classifying them and establishing relations between the classes thus defined. This misconception is not only an endemic error in modern philosophical thought about history, it is also a constant peril to historical thought itself."[10]

The positivist position was also characterized by an ardent commitment to the "realist" position. A realist's approach identifies certain "objectively" necessary features and holds that "whatever there is is what it is regardless of how we think of it."[11] Reality is viewed as independent of our minds and judgments. Therefore, judgments about reality are either true or false. Hilary Putnam says, "A distinguishing feature of the realistic sense of 'true' is it is logically possible for even the best attested statement to be false."[12] It can be falsified by something that is extrinsic to and independent of our minds. This views truth as being "out there" and as something that can be discovered. It should also be noted that "such a realist denies that what is essential to something (for example, knowledge) depends for its being essential on conceivers taking, or conceptualizing, it as essential."[13] The realist however acknowledges that some essences (such as essences of the perceiver) are dependent on the existence of the perceiver. The realist position has never been without a challenge from the various anti-realist

---

9. Collingwood, *The Idea of History*, 220.

10. Ibid., 228.

11. Cited by Evans, *Kierkegaard on Faith and the Self*, 30. Cf. Alston, "Yes, Virginia, There Is a Real World," 779.

12. Cited by Evans, *Kierkegaard on Faith and the Self*, 30. Cf. Putnam, "Realism and Reason," 485.

13. Moser, *Philosophy after Objectivity*, 21.

## Understanding Historical Religious Knowledge for Faith

positions. Since the time of Kant, idealism—the notion that everything that is knowable is mind-dependent—has been viewed as being the opposite of realism. Accordingly, if there is anything absolutely independent of the human mind, it cannot be known. Yet, idealism itself is not without criticism and is considered by some as "an error exclusively modern."[14]

With the questioning of the traditional approaches to history and their underlying assumptions, the biggest casualty has been the optimism surrounding historical inquiry. In a sense, the idealist view was a precursor to the twentieth-century hermeneutic of suspicion, visible in the Foucaultian understanding of history. For idealists like Collingwood and Dilthey, understanding history is to understand human actions by coming to know the inner motives and intentions of the agent, implying therefore that historical facts can never be divorced from historical interpretations. Thus, a historian using personal judgment and intuition arrives at historical facts "inferentially by a process of interpreting data according to a complicated system of rules and assumptions."[15] Accordingly, just as any historical account is intertwined with historical interpretations, the religious accounts of historical records are also inextricably intertwined with theological interpretation.

Among the variants to idealism, conceptualism holds that "essences depend for their being essences on a conceiver's taking them as essential, or as ontologically indispensable to the existence of a thing. It entails that something is an essence only if a conceiver takes it as such."[16] That is to say that an essence is what it is *only for* the conceiver: it implies asking "what is the essence of knowledge?" which is equivalent to asking, "What does the conceiver take as the essence of knowledge?"[17] Moser writes, "Conceptualism identifies a conceiver's activity (namely, conceptual taking, including dispositional psychological attitudes) as crucial to essences. . . . A realist might construe a description as an abstract item, such as a proposition. In that case, the active role of a conceiver gives a conceiver's activity a key role in essence-formation."[18]

Contrary to the realist idea of reality as standing totally independent from the conceiver, both idealism and conceptualism underscore the active

---

14. Adler, *The Four Dimensions of Philosophy*, 24.
15. Collingwood, *The Idea of History*, 133.
16. Moser, *Philosophy after Objectivity*, 23.
17. Ibid., 23.
18. Ibid., 23.

role of the conceiver. This is especially important in historical inquiry, where a historian inadvertently or consciously records only those events that are considered as 'essential' by him. Most importantly, this challenged the earlier view of history as an unbiased scrutiny of a natural succession of past events. A historian prefers certain events and excludes others. This necessitates that the writing of his text is toward a certain conclusion, which makes it impossible for him to distance himself from his writing.

Though not every form of anti-realism denies the "real world," they at least deny "that human language can refer to the world as it is in itself, apart from our human concepts and classifications, which in turn reflect our human activities and interests."[19] Such an anti-realist suspicion is not really about the things out there; rather it is a suspicion of the human ability to comprehend things as they are with finality, in line with Kant's affirmation of the reality of things-in-themselves, *Dinge an sich*, and the simultaneous dismissal of them as unknowable. Climacus' emphasis on subjectivity rather than objectivity in appropriating faith could portray him as an anti-realist.[20] However, the issue of whether Kierkegaard is or is not a realist definitely cannot be settled by a proof-text method because there are texts in the *Postscript* that can be used to argue either way.[21] Further, any anti-realism associated with Kierkegaard would have to consider his non-Socratic notion of self. That is to say, Climacus' subject does not create essence or possess it; in fact, he does not even have the condition to appropriate it within himself. Unlike the Socratic subject, who possesses the truth, or Lessing's rational subject who has the condition [rational religion], Climacus' individual has neither the truth nor the condition to avail it. It has to be introduced from without, by appropriating a God-ward relationship. However, as Evans clarifies:

> In all of this Kierkegaard seems to be committed to a kind of metaphysical realism. It is precisely the objectivity and mind-independent character of existent objects that makes knowledge of such objects uncertain in character. For example, Kierkegaard describes historical knowledge as "approximative" in character. But if our knowledge of history is approximative, this seems to imply that there is some kind of ideal to be approximated, and what else can

---

19. Evans, *Kierkegaard on Faith and the Self*, 30.

20. Evans lists various texts in CUP that lend themselves to both realist and anti-realist readings. See ibid., 31–33.

21. Evans, "Realism and Antirealism," 156.

*Understanding Historical Religious Knowledge for Faith*

such an ideal be but that of an accurate representation of the object of knowledge?²²

Anyhow, within the polarity of views on understanding the nature of historical data, Climacus seems to avoid the extremes. If one end of the polarity holds that there is no such thing as historical event that happens outside of an individual's life-world, entailing that there is no history *per se*, the other end of the polarity views history as science, purely objective, "no less and no more."²³ Climacus rejects both views.

## Understanding History through History

Historical events cannot be treated "as though they were physical objects, for that would assume that man has as little to do with the making of history as he has with the constitution of the object he examines in the laboratory."²⁴ Unlike objects, man is a part of history and there is no inquiry possible by distancing himself from it. History is one sphere where the objective and the subjective invariably interact. Having said this, one also cannot ignore the reality of historical events. As Rheinallt Nantlais Williams observes, "to bring light to the whole world, God chose to give it in the only way all could see it. The eternal donned the garments of time. Truth became embodied fact."²⁵

In *Postscript*, Climacus rejects the possibility of an observer seeing world history speculatively. However, in reality one does not look at history except through history.²⁶ As Climacus writes, "Insofar as the individuals participate in the history of the human race by their deeds, the observer does not see these deeds as traced back to the individuals and to the ethical but sees them as traced away from the individuals and to the totality."²⁷ Climacus sees history as a product of human deeds and not as something that one can speak of by distancing oneself from it. When history is seen as necessarily human deeds, then it is essentially a product of human interests

---

22. Evans, *Kierkegaard on Faith and the Self*, 40.
23. Williams cites J. B. Bury as holding this view. See, *Faith Facts History Science*, 86.
24. Ibid., 86.
25. Ibid., 80.
26. Collingwood, *The Idea of History*, 214.
27. CUP, 155.

or human intentions. Therefore, Climacus contends that history is primarily ethical in nature. He writes:

> Ethically, what makes the deed the individual's own is the intention, but this is precisely what is not included in world history, for here it is the world-historical intention that matters. World-historically, I see the effect; ethically, I see the intention. But when I ethically see the intention and understand the ethical, I also see that every effect is infinitely indifferent, that what the effect was is a matter of indifference, but then of course I do not see the world-historical.[28]

If human intentions are an essential part of history, then not only does the task of the historian become more difficult than that of the natural scientist, it also becomes different from his. The historian will have to recover the intentions of people. This can be done only by a complex process of re-enacting the past in the historian's own mind. As Collingwood writes, "The historian not only re-enacts past thought, he re-enacts in the context of his own knowledge and therefore, in re-enacting it, criticizes it, forms his own judgment of its value, corrects whatever errors he can discern in it. This criticism of the thought whose history he traces is not something secondary to tracing the history of it. It is an indispensable condition of the historical knowledge itself."[29]

A learner has the task of recovering truth about human intentions of the past events in question. Further, the learner has to do so from his own situatedness, a product of history himself—a condition that makes history doubly vulnerable. Uncertainty, which is characteristic of all human knowledge, is all the more pronounced in the case of historical knowledge. It is made uncertain, says Climacus, by virtue of the fact that the natural world is not a necessity but is contingent. Unlike the necessary, the natural world has "come into existence."[30] In addition to the natural world having come into existence, human actions make history doubly contingent, as human history involves the contingency of human intentions and actions. Historical evidencing, therefore, carries with it a contingency that makes it unreliable for the purpose of securing one's eternal happiness or faith. Thus, Kierkegaard thinks that a historical account of incarnation cannot become objective knowledge. The Enlightenment project's attempt to prevail over

---

28. CUP, 155.
29. Collingwood, *The Idea of History*, 215.
30. PF, 75–76.

historical contingency and gain a God's-eye-view is yet another instance of the original human fall, as an attempt to transcend createdness by "becoming like God."[31]

## Historical Critical Method and the Christian Faith

Appeals to the truth-value of historical Christian beliefs were not unique to the modernistic period. The first-century New Testament writers constantly appealed to the historicity of their beliefs and made their faith vulnerable to historical content,[32] although not necessarily to historical verification. However, the modern scientific approach, especially the positivist assumptions, gave a fresh impetus to the truth-claims of events in the New Testament, as it could now provide unshakable foundation for Christian faith. Thus developed, unique to Western Christianity, an affirmation of the positivist method, especially in response to the attack of higher criticisms launched against the Christian faith.

The historical critical method that arose with the renaissance/ reformation took new turns in the hands of those who were committed to naturalism. Their a priori rejection of the supernatural resulted in the already accentuated historical consciousness acquiring a naturalistic twist. The use of the historical critical method by empirical naturalists would expectably yield very different conclusions, where these conclusions (disturbing as they were to a believer) were intertwined with the method. Some orthodox Christians were ignorant of the fact that the conclusions of a naturalistic historian were primarily the outcome of certain rationalistic presuppositions rather than the method. This resulted in the rejection of not just the conclusions, but also of the method, by them. However, most of the conservative scholars now consider the value of the historical critical method, although divorced from its naturalistic assumptions. For a believer who credits a priori legitimacy to the Scriptures via inspiration, it is perfectly possible to factor in the concerns raised by historical and biblical criticism or situate the continuity of biblical authorship with the literary practices of its times, and yet see the hand of God in the process. In other words, it seems possible to acknowledge the role of the Holy Spirit whatever model one may subscribe to, in the formation of the Scriptures.

---

31. Gen 3:5.
32. 1 Cor 15:14–19.

## Truth and Subjectivity, Faith and History

Both the positivist approach (with a sense of certitude in the historicist method) and the anti-realist/ postmodern approaches (with the vagaries associated with it) have elicited corresponding responses from believing Christians. Just as the *zeitgeist* of a given historical period provides the endorsement to a given field of knowledge by laying down the epistemic parameters, the Enlightenment thinking brought about its compulsions. On the one hand, the religious adherents now sought scientific endorsement over matters of belief, which resulted in the quest for an alliance between Christian religious beliefs and existing scientific theories. On the other hand, they dissociated faith entirely from anything scientific. Kierkegaard's corrective seems to address both errors equally and simultaneously. Given that Christian beliefs are predominantly historical in nature, the positivist approach to history, which could deliver "objective" results, was readily welcomed by some Christians, opening the way for evidential apologetics. The evidentialist approach characteristically heightened the value of historical data, which became more appealing in the context of modern historicism, precisely because of the doubts raised by it. It was assumed that providing the certainty of scientific standards would help the cause of Christianity. At the same time, impacted by the vagaries of higher criticisms, some Christians dissociated history from Christian faith.

The Christian root of modern science has been successfully argued for. However, these connections were later severed, with the scientific community seeking greater autonomy from religion. The early connections between Christian faith and scientific rigor gave way to a scientific and historical inquiry that was not only autonomous from religious thinking, but also often in opposition to it in the modern period. A believer's approach to science thus led to, and was also influenced by, extensive, often bitter and embarrassing encounters with the scientific approaches, as in the case of the debates surrounding the theory of evolution.

This modern scientific attitude was characteristic of both the conservative and liberal thinkers. While the conservative theologian sought to prove the validity of Christian faith on the basis of historical inquiry, the liberal theologian, embarrassed by the presence of the "supernatural" in the biblical account, called for demythologizing the Scriptures. Rationalistic and naturalistic rejection of the supernatural—an error unique to the period—was inadvertently accepted as "rule" by most theologians. The German theologian, Ernst Troeltsch (1865–1923) remains a central figure in the shifts. As Mark Chan observes, "Troeltsch's rejection of revelational a priorism in favor of a historicized religious a priorism is not

## Understanding Historical Religious Knowledge for Faith

unlike the postmodern assault on authority and its emphasis on historical contingency."[33] Within the Troeltschian method, the "Bible is critically dissected like any other literary work, while miracles, once accepted as an indubitable foundation for belief, must be reappraised according to the principles of the historical method."[34] This view of the Scriptures also echoes in his theological stance, which Chan notes as "epistemological relativism: Christianity can be said to be true only in the sense of being 'true for' adherents of a particular social and cultural context."[35]

Bultmann's (1884–1976) criticism of biblical history unmasks his modernistic commitment. About the Bible, he complains, "History does not follow a smooth unbroken course, it is set in motion and controlled by these supernatural powers."[36] History, for him, should be an unbroken and natural chain of events that should be approached without biases. The modernistic commitment to history as a natural and continuous course could not accommodate the supernatural interventions within the religious traditions. However, on their part, religious believers predominantly did not view history as the unbroken chain of events, but rather accepted and even anticipated the supernatural as part of their worldview.

Instead of a total rejection of the supernatural, some theological responses sought to reconcile their faith with the vagaries associated with the historical method. It prompted some theologians to argue that religious faith should not depend on historical beliefs and should be devoid of historical content. For instance, dialectical theologians such as Paul Tillich conceived faith not as an assent to some specific historical propositions about Jesus, but rather as an "existential response" to the person of Christ, thus making a clear division between the "Jesus of history" and the "Christ of faith." Tillich considered faith as never compelled by knowledge and totally divorced from history. He argued, "Faith does not affirm or deny what belongs to the pre-scientific or scientific knowledge of our world. . . . The knowledge of our world (including ourselves as a part of our world) is a matter of inquiry by ourselves or by those in whom we trust. It is not a matter of faith. The dimension of faith is not the dimension of science, history or psychology. The acceptance of a probable hypothesis in these realms is

---

33. Chan, *Christology From Within and Ahead*, 21.
34. Ibid., 22.
35. Ibid., 32.
36. Bultmann, "New Testament and Mythology," 1.

not faith, but preliminary belief, to be tested by scholarly methods, and to be changed by every new discovery."[37]

Tillich, with a desire for an indubitable faith, protects it from history. For him, faith should not be linked to history, much less supported by it. The reason is that when linked to history, one's faith will have to share the skepticism surrounding history. Where faith has no empirical content, it remains above the possibility of a scholar proving some part of the empirical content wrong. For thinkers such as Tillich, the pursuit for certainty with regard to matters of faith would destroy it; although, ironically, it is the pursuit for certainty that tries to insulate faith from history.

C. Stephen Evans in his book, *Kierkegaard on Faith and the Self*, rightly records a trend, especially within the liberal traditions, where words such as "incarnation," "resurrection," and "salvation" are reinterpreted to mean entirely different ideas, including those ideas that were meant to be excluded from the original understanding of the terms. Evans calls it "misusing religious language" when, say, a theologian explains "resurrection" as someone continuing "to exist not only in God's memory but in God's ongoing work in the world; he is 'resurrected' in other people's lives and in God's everlasting consciousness."[38] This conscious betrayal of the original meaning where "belief in the resurrection can be taken as excluding or denying that Jesus remained dead past the time of his resurrection or that he is now dead"[39] amounts to misusing religious language.

It was against this overriding liberal theological *zeitgeist* in Europe, that Kierkegaard brings to focus the centrality of incarnation to the Christian faith. For Kierkegaard, theological liberalism eliminates the central features of Christianity—the possibility of offence and the location of truth outside the individual, both of which are uniquely presented in the incarnation. Thus, Climacus presents incarnation as the "absolute paradox" providing the maximal possibility of offence, comparable to "capital crime" that "absorbs all lesser crimes" such as the claims about various miracles. Yet, it is not the idea of incarnation that causes the offence, but Christ. Since incarnation involves God becoming human and eternity entering history, it supports Climacus' argument for the uniqueness of Christianity vis-à-vis any other religion or philosophical thinking situating truth as external to humans. Theological liberalism eliminates the possibility of offence

---

37. Tillich, *The Dynamics of Faith*, 33.
38. Evans, *Kierkegaard on Faith and the Self*, 99.
39. Ibid., 98.

by reinterpreting the belief in the bodily resurrection or the virgin birth within mythological categories. It also reverts to Socratic thinking in that it inadvertently locates the truth within the individual, who assumes the position of the arbiter, functioning purely within naturalistic and rationalistic assumptions.

Undoubtedly, the appearance of the eternal God in history presents certain problems for human reason that functions purely within naturalistic assumptions. The historical nature of Christian beliefs raises specific concerns. Can faith be based on history? What is the connection between eternal truth and history? Is a historical dimension crucial for the Christian faith? Is it possible to reconcile faith and our concern for accurate history? Kierkegaard addresses issues such as these in his pseudonymous work *Philosophical Fragments* and thus becomes an excellent candidate who can help provide clarity to the interface between Christian faith and historical inquiry.

Naturally, no historical belief can have religious significance by merely being a historical belief; it must have something more. Religious beliefs in general and Christian beliefs in particular contain beliefs pertaining to human origin, destiny, purpose, and salvation. A Christian believes in certain historical facts, such beliefs as: God became man; he lived and performed many miracles; he died, and was bodily raised from the dead. These beliefs inevitably go beyond the realm of the natural into the supernatural and consequently raise genuine problems, especially for someone who allows only the natural, on the question of faith's relation to historical research. But as Stephen Evans rightly cautions, one should not argue that some "genuine problems that make historical religious knowledge difficult" make "such knowledge impossible."[40]

Murray Rae argues that the reasons for today's lower estimation of historical knowledge lie in the varied nuances that Western historiography has undergone, particularly after the Enlightenment.[41] As Rae shows, "the negative estimation of history that is the precursor to Lessing's problem, has its roots in Platonism but reemerges in the philosophy of Spinoza (1632–77) and Leibniz (1646–1716) both of whose writings are counted amongst Lessing's favorite philosophical reading."[42] Gotthold E. Lessing (1729–81), to whom I shall return in the next chapter, argued that con-

---

40. Evans, "Empiricism, Rationalism, and the Possibility," 136.
41. Rae, "The Forgetfulness of Historical-Talkative Remembrance," 72.
42. Rae, "The Forgetfulness of Historical-Talkative Remembrance," 73.

tingent historical truths can never match the necessary truths of reason. Even earlier, Plato had conceived that true knowledge cannot be gained by perception through the senses; only through abstract and systematic reasoning, as in the case of mathematics can one arrive at it. Spinoza reiterated this Platonic thinking when he wrote, "The truth of a historical narrative, however assured, cannot give us the knowledge nor consequently the love of God, for love of God springs from knowledge of God, and knowledge of God should be derived from general ideas, in themselves certain and known, so that the truth of a historical narrative is very far from being a necessary requisite for our attaining our highest good."[43] Likewise, Leibniz argued that "truths of reason are necessary and their opposite is impossible; those of fact are contingent and their opposite is possible."[44] This thinking that regarded the historical as an inauthentic means for knowledge (*nous*) and understanding (*episteme*) forms the precursor to not only the separation of the historical Jesus and the Christ of faith, but also to the post-Enlightenment confounding of history and myth.

## Climacus on the Limits of a Critical Theologian

Climacus distinguishes between the task of a philologist and the task of a critical theologian. The philologist's undertaking, Climacus argues, which is to give a text the most accurate examination possible, "is wholly legitimate, and the present author certainly has respect, second to none, for that which scholarship consecrates."[45] A philological inquiry surely has its place and deserves our "admiration." However, "it has no bearing on faith."[46] On the other hand, a critical theologian—a Troeltsch, or a Bultmann, or a Hick—errs in overstepping his boundary to conclude that Scriptures are not authoritative. For Climacus, historical scholarship cannot prove or disprove the veracity of faith and its content. On the question of authority, pointing to the distinction in the categories involved, Kierkegaard writes that when he draws *the difference between a Genius and an Apostle*, "It is nonsense to obtain *physical* certainty that an Apostle is an Apostle (the paradoxical qualification of a relation of spirit), just as it is nonsense to obtain *physical*

---

43. Cited by Rae, ibid. Cf. Spinoza, *Tractatus theologico-politicus*, iv.

44. Cited by Rae, "The Forgetfulness of Historical-Talkative Remembrance," 73. Cf. Leibniz, *Monadology and Other Philosophical Writings*, §33, 236.

45. CUP, 25.

46. CUP, 28.

certainty that God exists, since God is *spirit*."⁴⁷ Revelation then is received not by an ordinary witness, but by an apostle. Thus revelation cannot be claimed by an ordinary witness, but can be claimed by an apostle. For a Christian, "events are explicable on two levels," says J. H. Whittaker: "The level of natural causes and the level of supernatural causes, they are without the means to justify this distinction. The same applies even in the case of miracles, or events for which a natural explanation cannot be found and for which a supernatural explanation is supposedly required. Historians can never *justify* the claim that a miracle, or a supernaturally caused event, has occurred. They can only acknowledge a bare event and confess their lack of any explanation, saying only, 'This event has occurred; we do not know why; we cannot explain it.'"⁴⁸

If a critical theologian is out of bounds to negate Christian faith purely from within historical research, he also errs in applying textual criticism to the Scriptures, and "when finished—and until then it holds us *in suspenso*, but with this very prospect in mind—it concludes: *ergo*, now you can build your eternal happiness on these writings."⁴⁹ Therefore, according to Climacus,

> Whoever defends the Bible with regard to faith must certainly have made clear to himself whether all his work, if it succeeded according to the highest expectations, would result in something in that respect, lest he become stuck in the parenthesis of his labor and, amid the difficulties of scholarship, forget the decisive dialectical *claudatur* [let it be closed]. Whoever attacks must likewise have reckoned whether the attack, if it succeeded on the largest possible scale, would result in something other than the philological result, or at most in a victory by contending *e concessis*, in which, please note, one can lose everything in a different way, that is, if the mutual agreement is illusory.⁵⁰

From a historical standpoint, one can be reasonably certain about the life of Jesus, who, according to the New Testament writers, claimed to be divine. The truth of that claim, however, is beyond the scope of historical scholarship. The New Testament writer only witnesses to the truth and does not try to prove it. Kierkegaard is of the view that the critical theologian

---

47. WA, 98.
48. Whittaker, "Kierkegaard on History and Faith," 386.
49. CUP, 26.
50. CUP, 28.

who says, "we have stacked up the evidence and ergo belief is imminent," tries to prove what is out of bounds for him. It is the synthesis of the God-man, the eternal-temporal, and the transcendent-immanent in incarnation, that makes faith unattainable for the critical theologian because even his "most consummate fulfillment would still remain an approximation."[51] This is because all his investigations are within the categories of immanence. The most that the critical theologian can assert is that "it is as if every letter is inspired."

Besides being fundamentally shaped by a historical consciousness, a historian works with empirical data obtained from manuscripts, book inscriptions, archaeological reports, coins, archive materials and the history of languages, without which there is no history. The historian is also a witness to the New Testament writer's witnesses. His task is to make meaningful interpretations of all this data. However, can there be solid empirical data for the transcendental aspects of Christian faith, data that will settle all issues once and for all? Can certainty eliminate uncertainty through approximation? Climacus answers, no! If some thinkers have tried to prove the transcendental facets of the Christian faith through historical inquiry, some others have tried to disprove the same on historical grounds. However, such an undertaking is erroneous because there is no evidence which can be accessed by historians to support the transcendental accounts of the Christian faith. Such a quest, according to Murray Rae, "represents neither the failure of historical method nor the falsification of Christian faith but rather a simple category mistake on the part of those who make such claims."[52] As Climacus argues, "It is easy for the contemporary learner to become a historical eyewitness, but the trouble is that knowing a historical fact—indeed, knowing all the historical facts with the trustworthiness of an eyewitness—by no means makes the eyewitness a follower, which is understandable, because such knowledge means nothing more to him than the historical."[53] For Climacus, the problem with the veracity of the Scriptures on which the truth of Christian beliefs depends, is that they are historical documents and "that as soon as it is made the stronghold an introductory approximation commences, and the subject is diverted into a parenthesis, the conclusion of which one awaits for all eternity."[54] The truth

51. CUP, 30.
52. Rae, "Kierkegaard and the Historians," 89.
53. PF, 59.
54. CUP, 38.

about Christianity and the veracity of the Scriptures are convincing only to a believer. For an unbeliever, not only is the same data unappealing, but it can also become an instrument to attack Christian beliefs.

One of the major difficulties surrounding historical religious beliefs concerns miracles and the testimony to the miraculous. Christian beliefs not only include the acceptance of the miraculous in the past, but also persuade a believer to anticipate them in their present lives. Conversely, a naturalist who a priori rejects the supernatural also rejects with it, the possibility of a miracle. I shall briefly consider the objection to miracles by the British empiricist David Hume (1711–76) and the modern British philosopher, Antony Flew (1923–2010).

## Miracles and Historical Religious Belief

### Miracles and Faith

The question of miracles elicits varied responses depending on one's pretheoretical commitment. If one proceeds from an a priori belief in the supernatural, one would not be surprised by the supernatural interventions that such a belief would allow. Conversely, a naturalist would find such interventions impossible also because of the a priori commitment to naturalism and therefore would also find claims about supernatural interventions doubtful. Naturally, once the possibility of the supernatural and the miraculous is ruled out, the debate is reduced merely to claims and testimonies about miracles, rather than the miracles themselves.

In his essay on miracles, in part 10 of the *Enquiry Concerning Human Understanding*, David Hume speaks of whether or not a testimony is sufficient to establish a miracle. He rightly distinguishes between the testimony of an ordinary event and that of a miracle. Hume holds that, in the case of an ordinary event, to conceive the falsity of what is sought to be established would be more miraculous than the fact itself. In such cases, a testimony is sufficient. But, he further argues that "a miracle is a violation of a law of nature . . . and unalterable experience has established these laws . . ."[55] To find as false a claim made by someone, however surprising it may be, does not violate any law of nature as there is no law of nature that states, "everything anyone believes should be true." Two implications follow from Humean thinking. First, by reducing the question on miracles to claims of

55. Cited by Geisler, *Miracles and Modern Thought*, 27. Cf. Hume, *Inquiry*, 10. 1. 122.

people about miracles, Hume betrays his a priori rejection of miracles, thus circumventing the real issue, which is, whether miracles are possible. Second, his thinking implies that it is more probable that a person is mistaken rather than that a miracle he reports has happened. For Hume, miracles as violations of the laws of nature, "have maximal improbability, or they would not be miracles at all."[56] That is, for an occurrence to be described as a "miracle," it would have to stand out against "uniform experience." "Otherwise the event would not merit that appellation." Hence, "nothing is esteemed a miracle if it ever happened in the common course of nature."[57]

Hume's argument against miracles is faulty in the way he sets it up. Functionally, he employs a circular reasoning by defining miracles as impossible as they "by definition are violations of natural law and natural laws are unalterably uniform," an interpretation Norman Geisler calls "the hard interpretation."[58] This interpretation, which is essentially a rationalistic a priori rejection of the possibility of miracles, contradicts his empiricist commitment. That is, if Hume were to be true to his empiricist commitment, he ought not to define miracles as impossible before their occurrence, since miraculous events are essentially empirical claims that demand empirical verification rather than rationalistic repudiation.

Further however, one could very well point out that miracles are not "violations" of any natural law. Even if they were, natural laws are not established on the basis of any a priori rationalistic understanding but on empirical experience. As Hume himself argues, "All inferences from experience, therefore, are effects of custom, not of reasoning . . ."[59] Here Hume is being inconsistent, in arguing that natural laws such as causality—which are neither based on reasoning nor empirical grounding, are unalterably uniform so that no other possibility is allowed.

There is however a "soft interpretation" of Hume's argument that Geisler finds more probable: "It is not an argument for the impossibility of miracles but for the *incredibility* of miracles."[60] Geisler states this in the following steps: "a) A miracle is by definition a rare occurrence. b) Natural law is by definition a description of a regular occurrence. c) The evidence

---

56. Ward, "Miracles and Testimony," 132.

57. Cited by Geisler, *Miracles and Modern Thought*, 27. Cf. Hume, *Inquiry*, 10. 1. 122–23.

58. Geisler, *Miracles and Modern Thought*, 27–29.

59. Hume, *Inquiry*, 5. 1. 57.

60. Geisler, *Miracles and Modern Thought*, 28.

for the regular is always greater than that for the rare. d) A wise man always bases his belief on the greater evidence. e) Therefore, a wise man should never believe in miracles."⁶¹ But the question is, what is greater evidence? For a believer who regards God as the creator who controls and often intervenes in the world, there is greater evidence for believing in miracles. Conversely, for an unbeliever, even if there were a miracle, he would not be in a position to see it, for he has ruled out the possibility of the same prior to his encounter of it. Hume's "wise man" is therefore a determination that has no real bearing on the examination of any empirical evidence.

Hume seems to theoretically allow for the possibility of miracles in the first premise and takes a seemingly empiricist's position. However, he practically falls into a rationalistic denial whereby no "wise man" can ever believe that a miracle has indeed occurred. Geisler is right in pointing out that even the soft interpretation presents us with at least two problems. He explains it by analyzing Hume's phrase "uniform experience." Geisler observes that this "either begs the question or else is special pleading. It begs the question if Hume presumes to know the experience is uniform *in advance* of looking at the evidence. For how can one know that all *possible* experience will confirm his naturalism, unless he has access to all possible experiences, including those in the future? If, on the other hand, Hume simply means by "uniform" experience that select experiences of *some* persons (who have not encountered a miracle), then this is special pleading. For there are others who claim to have experienced miracles."⁶² Similarly, exposing the circularity in Hume's argument of uniform experience, C. S. Lewis writes,

> Now of course we must agree with Hume that if there is absolutely "uniform experience" against miracles, if in other words they have never happened, why then they never have. Unfortunately we know the experience against them to be uniform only if we know that all the reports of them are false. And we can know all the reports to be false only if we know already that miracles have never occurred. In fact, we are arguing in a circle. The only alternative to this circular arguing is to be open to the possibility that miracles have occurred.⁶³

---

61. Ibid., 28.
62. Ibid., 29.
63. Lewis, *Miracles*, 105.

Unless one is self-restricted by certain pre-theoretical commitments, one is open to the possibility of experiences that may not be anticipated. As Keith Ward rightly summarizes, "we place a very high reliance on the testimony of the senses; we regard them as trustworthy, unless there is very good reason to distrust them, in particular cases."[64] That is, even if the event witnessed were a highly unlikely one, one would rather trust one's own senses than rest the case on the improbability of its occurrence.

Let me turn to another type of expectation, that of "repeatability" that is thrust upon unique empirical events such as miracles. According to Antony Flew, Hume "was primarily concerned, not with the question of fact, but with evidence. The problem was how the occurrence of a miracle could be proved, rather than whether any such events had ever occurred."[65] Flew's rejection of miracles is on the basis of the unrepeatability of such events, which according to him make the alleged miracles scientifically impossible. He says, "For it is only and precisely by presuming that the laws that hold today held in the past . . . that we can rationally interpret the *detritus* [fragments] of the past as evidence and from it construct our account of what actually happened."[66] He further says, "The propositions reporting the (alleged) occurrence of the miracle will be singular, particular, and in the past tense," which "cannot any longer be tested directly. It is this that gives propositions of the first sort [i.e., of the general and repeatable] the vastly greater logical strength . . ."[67]

First, Flew's argument for repeatability is unwarranted. The repeatability principle is sought only to establish a law that will enable us to seek instantiations for that law in our empirical observations. Miracles, by Humean definition, which Flew seems to accept, are occurrences that violate natural law, or a believer may understand them as exceptions to natural occurrences. Hence, Hume ought not to expect the same miraculous event to be repeated, for then it would cease to be a miracle. Secondly, repeatability cannot be necessitated even in proving ordinary historical events. There is compelling evidence for some unrepeatable things of the past. For example, evidence for the two World Wars is more compelling than some repeatable occurrence in the present, like a chess player defeating a computer at his own game. Hume and Flew seem to use the singularity of miracles as an

---

64. Ward, "Miracles and Testimony," 132.

65. Cited by Geisler, *Miracles and Modern Thought*, 36.

66. Cited by Geisler, ibid., 37. Cf. Flew, "Miracles." It should be noted that Antony Flew later repudiated his original naturalism and believed in some form of a god.

67. Cited by Geisler, *Miracles and Modern Thought*, 37. Cf. Flew, "Miracles."

*Understanding Historical Religious Knowledge for Faith*

argument against them. According to Geisler, it is evident that, "Most modern naturalists, such as Flew, accept some irrepeatable singularities of their own. Many contemporary astronomers believe in the singular origin of the universe by a 'Big Bang.' And nearly all scientists believe that the origin of life on this planet is a singular event that has never been repeated here. . . . Thus Flew's argument against supernaturalism would also eliminate some basic naturalistic belief(s)."[68]

Objection to particular claims of miracles on grounds that are relevant to the situation is possible. However, objection to miracles based on an a priori rejection of its possibility, makes it a rationalistic rejection that is not even open to the possibility of miracles. This proves nothing more than the bias of the individual holding "an a priori conception of the nature of religious knowledge or of historical knowledge or both."[69] From the above discussion, we can glean two dominant approaches in Western philosophy that have had definite impact on one's approach to historical religious beliefs—the rationalist and the empiricist approaches, to which I shall now turn.

## The Rationalist and the Empiricist Conceptions

A rationalist's primary functioning scheme is reason. Along Platonic lines, he believes that, given the human cognitive structure, religious truths are not only self-evident and necessary truths but also timeless and eternal. The nature of "human cognitive structure" is pivotal as knowledge is mediated through human reason. As Evans clarifies, "the features of human nature in question may not be logically necessary, religious truths of this type are not strictly necessary, but they resemble necessary truths in that they cannot be altered unless human beings were altered to become radically different kinds of beings."[70]

The empiricist, on the other hand, accepts or rejects historical religious beliefs on the basis of experience or empirical confirmation. However, at least in principle, his position is open to the possibility of historical religious knowledge, as there is no a priori value judgment on its possibility. Conversely, the empiricist would hold that the rejection of the possibility of

---

68. Geisler, *Miracles and Modern Thought*, 38.
69. Evans, "Empiricism, Rationalism, and the Possibility," 140.
70. Ibid., 137.

historical religious knowledge in principle is to hold "an a priori conception of the nature of religious knowledge or of historical knowledge or both."[71]

The problem however, Evans maintains, is when the two objections (rationalist and empiricist) are confused. He refers to Van Harvey's critique of Rudolf Bultmann as a case in point, where Bultmann is accused of "illegitimately dragging in empirical content when his operative understanding of religious knowledge is rationalist."[72] Van Harvey writes, "this reference to a decisive act of God in Jesus Christ seems gratuitous within the framework of Bultmann's theology. For him, Jesus is merely the historical cause (*das Dass*), which initiates faith. The figure of Jesus does not inform in any way the content (*das Was*) of faith. Moreover, this reference to Jesus not only seems unnecessary but contradictory, since it is impossible to reconcile with Bultmann's basic premise that faith is a possibility for man as man."[73] Evans argues that critics of historically derived religious knowledge often make a mistake similar to Bultmann. The problem surrounding historical religious knowledge can be summarized in his words: "They raise objections to historical religious knowledge that are apparently empirical in nature, and thus presuppose an empiricist conception of religious knowledge that is open in principle to such historical knowledge. When we look more deeply, however, we find that these empirical objections are a smoke screen for covert rationalist presuppositions. Legitimate empirical problems then lend unwarranted support for the covert rationalism. Alternatively, the covert rationalism is employed to portray the empirical difficulties as being insuperable, impossible to overcome, instead of simply being difficulties."[74]

For someone who uses naturalism as the operative presupposition, there is hardly any evidence for the supernatural and the miraculous because that possibility simply does not exist. Unlike the naturalist, Kierkegaard sets his response in the way he defines human beings. One's understanding of the nature of human beings defines his response to the problem. Defining a human being as a spirit, Anti-Climacus writes, "A human being is a synthesis of the infinite and the finite, of the temporal and the eternal, of freedom and necessity, in short a synthesis."[75] Central to this definition is the locating of the human beings within the realm that interfaces these

71. Ibid., 140.
72. Ibid., 141.
73. Harvey, *The Historian and the Believer*, 165.
74. Evans, "Empiricism, Rationalism, and the Possibility," 141.
75. SUD, 13.

opposing categories. This anti-naturalist definition of what a human being is sets the tone for integrating eternal virtues of truth, beauty, and morality, which are based on such a synthesis and also the entire Kierkegaardian understanding of Christian faith. Kierkegaardian view of humans as a synthesis is all the more decisive for his view on incarnation, where the convergence of opposing categories is seen as the absolute paradox.

## Kierkegaard on the Miraculous

Keeping Spinoza in mind, Kierkegaard writes in *Eighteen Upbuilding Discourses*: "There was a thinker, much admired in memory, who taught that miracle was a characteristic of the Jewish people, that in a characteristic way this people leaped over the intervening causes to reach God."[76] The same issue is addressed in *Journals and Papers*, where he writes: "Strange that Spinoza continually objects to miracles and revelation on the ground that it was a Jewish trait to lead something directly back to God and leap over the intermediate causes, just as if this were a peculiarity only of the Jews and not of all religiousness, so that Spinoza himself would have done so if he had been basically religious, and as if the difficulty did not lie right here: whether, to what extent, how—in short, inquiries which could give the keenest thinking enough to do."[77] Likewise, in *Works of Love*, Kierkegaard talks about how "faith always relates itself to what is not seen." A person "by faith *believes* the *unseen into* ['til' is in bold-face in the original] what is seen." The most explicit statement is however that "the miracle of faith happens (and every miracle [Mirakel] is then a miracle of faith—no wonder, therefore, that along with faith miracles [Miraklerne] also have been abolished!)"[78] Therefore, both Kierkegaard and Climacus hold that one's idea of miracles/historical religious beliefs is directly linked to one's idea of faith.

Without engaging in a direct defense of the miraculous *per se*, Kierkegaard presupposes that once the miraculous is removed, there really remains no Christianity. The Christian faith involves beliefs of not only ordinary historical occurrences, but also of extraordinary occurrences, such as miracles. Elaborating upon the extent of the extraordinariness, Kierkegaard contrasts the birth of Jesus with that of John the Baptist in *Eighteen*

76. EUD, 243.
77. JP, 2: 1333.
78. WL, 295.

*Upbuilding Discourses.* Kierkegaard says that the origin of John the Baptist was "As marvelous [*vidunderlig*] as the origin of the one whose coming he proclaimed, but the difference here again was the same as the difference between the marvel [*Vidunderlige*] that an aged woman becomes pregnant, which is contrary to the order of nature [*mod Naturens Orden*], and that a pure virgin bears a child by the power of God, which is above the order of nature [*over Naturens Orden*]."[79]

Further, in his *Journal* Kierkegaard writes, "the highest collisions, [are] where the expected is altogether opposed to the order of nature [*mod Naturens Orden*] (for example, that Sara gets a child although far beyond the natural age to bear children)."[80] Kierkegaard maintains a distinction between that which is "contrary to the order of nature" and that which is "above the order of nature." Jyrki Kivela observes that, for Kierkegaard, "The 'truly miraculous' refers to an event which violates the established order of nature, and the 'merely marvelous' refers to an event which is very unusual and surprising, but does not violate the established order of nature."[81] While both the birth of Jesus and that of Isaac are not ordinary events, the former refers to "the 'truly miraculous' as something very exceptional, which violates or transgresses the order of nature—that is, like 'a pure virgin' bearing a child by 'the power of God.'" Whereas Sara having a baby refers to "something very rare and surprising but still belongs to the natural realm of things."[82] However, neither Kierkegaard nor Climacus seem to think that the truly miraculous *violates the established order of nature* in the real sense, though it may be against common understanding. By preferring the term "above" over against the term "violation," Kierkegaard seems to suggest that there is a higher order, which is above the "natural order" and can be understood only spiritually.

In *Three Discourses at the Communion on Fridays*, Kierkegaard writes, "no gaze is as sharp-sighted, as that of faith, and yet faith, humanly speaking, is blind; reason, understanding, is, humanly speaking, sighted, but faith is against the understanding."[83] Natural laws, it may be noted, are established

---

79. EUD, 277. It should be pointed out that *"vidunder,"* which Hong translates as "marvel," can also be translated as "miracle."

80. JP, 3:3130.

81. Kivela, "Kierkegaard on Miracles," 14.

82. Ibid., 12.

83. WA, 132.

by observation or experience or custom, and not by a priori reasoning.[84] Conversely, Kierkegaard suggests that it is natural for a believer to expect a miracle, which in this case, is merely God's intervention in the created world. It would therefore be more appropriate to use Kierkegaard's term "above" rather than "violation" as Jyrki Kivela maintains.

## Conclusion

The purpose of this chapter has been to serve as an introductory discussion to the specific issues surrounding history and faith. As in the case of truth-discourses, one's pre-theoretical commitment is central in informing judgments on historical religious beliefs. Besides the popular views about history influencing religious beliefs, I have specifically noted how rationalistic biases can influence views, even an empiricist's view, about historical religious beliefs. These biases often inform how miracles, which are a type of historical religious beliefs, are viewed.

While not every miracle or testimony of a miracle needs to be affirmed within the historical Christian beliefs, it is nonetheless pivotal to affirm the possibility of miracles. First, the advent of Christ affirms eternity entering history and the related beliefs thereof are inherently claims of the miraculous in history. Second, the advent of the Holy Spirit that causes sanctification in the individual is an inherent claim about the miraculous in the personal life of a believer. How then can the miraculous make sense in a natural world? For Kierkegaard, a believer's spiritual eyes that are opened by the moment of faith, are open to the belief not only about the advent of Christ in history but also to the advent of the Holy Spirit in his life. This implies that a naturalist cannot see the miraculous as he is devoid of the spiritual eyes needed for an autopsy of faith. This conclusion informs the central Climacean question, "can it be demonstrated from history that Christ was God?" which I shall discuss in the next chapter.

---

84. This is Humean understanding too. cf. Hume, *Inquiry*, 5. 1. 57.

# 5

# Historical Research and Its Sufficiency for Faith

*Can a historical point of departure be given for an eternal consciousness? how can such a point of departure be of more than historical interest? can an eternal happiness be built on historical knowledge?* — PF, TITLE PAGE.

FOLLOWING A GENERAL DISCUSSION pertaining to historical religious knowledge for faith in the last chapter, I shall discuss in this one, a specifically Kierkegaardian approach, which I believe provides a balance between the various polarities while integrating Christian faith and the concern for accurate history. The Kierkegaardian approach avoids the error of rejecting the miraculous, as instanced by naturalists and by some liberal theologians, who dismiss the supernatural interventions as unreal myths that are to be eliminated. Further, it avoids the dialectical theologian's conception of faith as purely an existential response to Christ rather than to the historical Jesus. Thirdly, it shuns the opportunistic approach of evidential apologetics, which uses positivistic calculus to establish Christian faith on historical evidence.

Kierkegaard's Christian presuppositions allow him to accept the miraculous as part of a believer's experience when viewed through the "autopsy of faith." More pertinently, we learn through Climacean insights how one could avoid both a total disregard for the historical (as in the case of the dialectical theologian), and the type of apologetics that is overly dependent on historical data (as in the case of the evidential apologist). To illustrate these insights, I shall look at how (in Climacus' account) the historical is decisive for Christian faith, while historical data fails to qualify as evidence that can generate faith. I shall also discuss the role and usefulness of evidence for faith. Then I shall dwell on Climacus' views on the contemporaneity of a believer with Christ in response to Lessing, who finds the contemporary individual distanced by an insurmountably broad and ugly temporal ditch from the first century. Lessing's problem is shared by many an individual who misunderstands the nature of Christian faith even today.

## On the Decisiveness of History for Christian Faith

In *Philosophical Fragments* Climacus delineates the contrast between the Socratic and the Christian ways of obtaining eternal truth. The Socratic view posits truth as being entirely immanent, located within the individual, discovered by recollection, and mediated by the Socratic teacher. On the other hand, the Christian view locates truth external to the individual, which necessitates that it to be given by the ultimate teacher, God himself. Climacus opines that while Socrates deserves the highest esteem for his understanding, his position becomes intrinsically superfluous and ethically offensive after the advent of Christ.

The incarnation of Christ then forms the focal point for the entry of the eternal God into history. Consequently this presents the temporal individual with the possibility of encountering the eternal. Downplaying the historical would then violate the essential character of Christian faith. In fact, it is the moment of incarnation that makes faith even possible. "In the moment of faith," Mark C. Taylor points out, "the sinner (the temporal self) is saved (becomes eternal). Faith is, thus, the inverse image of the Incarnation. In the incarnation the Eternal becomes temporal but remains eternal; in the moment of faith, the sinner realizes the possibility of eternal blessedness (immortality), but remains temporal."[1]

This historical point of departure gives the Christian faith its decisive feature, where, "god appeared in the humble form of a servant, lived and taught among us, and then died."[2] The form of a servant and the state of abasement, which is the highest form of *kenosis*, were not merely a disguise to generate devotion; rather, it amounts to an eternal sacrifice. Hence

---

1. Taylor, *Kierkegaard's Pseudonymous Authorship*, 10.
2. PF, 104. The theme of *kenosis* is epitomized in Phil 2:5–11, an early Christian hymn.

Climacus writes, Christ "has himself become captive, so to speak, in his resolution and is now obliged to continue (to go on talking loosely) whether he wants to or not. He cannot betray his identity."[3] In other words, Christ's incarnation into the historical has not only a historical significance, but also an eternal significance—one becomes a believer and thus enters eternity only by encountering God in his humanity, in his abasement.[4] The object of Christian faith is therefore the historical Christ, who appeared and lived in space and time, and stands in contrast to an imagined, mythological being.

Conversely, "if the god did not come himself, then everything would remain Socratic,"[5] where truth is arrived at by looking inward, making explicit that which was implicit in the form of latent memory. In the Socratic mode, "The teacher is only an occasion, whoever he may be, even if he is a god, because only when *I* discover it is it discovered, not before, even though the whole world knew it."[6] Climacus, therefore, dissociates the Christian understanding from the subjectivism inherent in Socratic thinking, although Socrates himself may not be accused of it. Further, as Pojman points out, in the Socratic scheme, "The Moment of discovery of Truth is accidental. The opportunity is always available. You must merely use your innate ability to discover it,"[7] which entails that self-knowledge and God-knowledge are identical.[8]

Climacus' emphasis on the uniqueness of the Christian faith is further clarified by distinguishing between the existence-spheres—religiousness A and religiousness B. Once again, this distinction fundamentally rests on the historical point of departure instanced in the moment of the incarnation that Christianity confesses to unlike other beliefs. As Calvin O. Schrag observes, "In religiousness A the movement is from self to God, finding God in the depths of the self. In the religiousness B the movement is from God to the self."[9] The God-ward movement of religiousness A, following the Socratic location of truth within the self, attempts to search and find god/godliness within immanence, as it is fundamentally an effort of the

---

3. PF, 55. This echoes the biblical description of the lamb that was slain eternally, who bears the marks on him. Cf. Rev 5:6, 12; 13:8.

4. PC, 24.

5. PF, 55.

6. PF, 14.

7. Pojman, "Kierkegaard on Faith and History," 58.

8. PF, 11.

9. Schrag, "The Kierkegaard-Effect," 10.

## Historical Research and Its Sufficiency for Faith

individual self. Religiousness A is the "religion of immanence," where the existential self appropriates the truth of the God-relationship through the dialectic of inwardness. On the other hand, religiousness B, as Schrag observes, "punctuates the decisive moment in the life of the existence-spheres by marking out the advent of the incursion of the eternal into the temporal, the descent of the divine into the historical, disclosing the ground of edification in a source other than that of the self."[10]

This moment of incarnation is the *kairotic* moment in that it is also the moment of salvation, thus transpiring as the "fullness of time" and not merely as the ordinary *chronotic*[11] moment. It is in the *kairotic* moment that "when the time had fully come, God sent forth his Son, born of woman, born under the law, to redeem those who were under the law, so that we might receive adoption as sons."[12] That "moment" in time is decisive because it is no ordinary moment but is "filled with the eternal." The question: "How can something historical become decisive for an eternal happiness?" has that paradoxical *kairotic* moment as the answer. The paradox is that God was in time; the eternal was in history. It is *kairotic* in that the decisive action is on the part of God and not man. Climacus writes in *Fragments*: "A moment such as this is unique. To be sure, it is short and temporal, as the moment is; it is passing, as the moment is, past, as the moment is in the next moment and yet it is decisive, and yet it is filled with the eternal. A moment such as this must have a special name. Let us call it: the *fullness of time*."[13]

The significance of the moment of incarnation is also that it is the *most decisive moment* for faith. It has been suggested that Climacus speaks of two distinct moments: the "moment of incarnation" and the "moment of faith."[14] It has also been suggested that "they are two aspects of the same moment, since incarnation is only a reality for those who have faith."[15] To view the "moment of incarnation" as distinct from the "moment of faith" is to consider the incarnation as an event that stands by itself, irrespective of how it is perceived. The contra-distinction that Climacus draws from the

---

10. Schrag, "The Kierkegaard-Effect," 10.
11. *Chronos* refers to the ordinary, mundane use of the term "time."
12. Gal 4:4–5.
13. PF, 18.
14. Taylor, *Kierkegaard's Pseudonymous Authorship*, 291ff.
15. Emmanuel, *Kierkegaard and the Concept of Revelation*, 64. Cf. Muller, *Meddelelsensdialektik i Søren Kierkegaards Philosophiske Smuler*, 41.

Socratic stance, where "only when *I* discover it is it discovered, not before, even though the whole world knew it,"[16] is not so much to present Socrates as an anti-realist; rather, it is to point out that the absence of incarnation necessitates the Socratic position to locate truth within the individual. However, Climacus seems to suggest that the "moment of incarnation" is not only distinct but also something that generates the "moment of faith" in the individual, as "the god's presence is not incidental to his teaching but is essential."[17] Therefore, for Climacus, faith is established not by an ahistorical contemplative process of looking inward, but by an encounter with the historical Jesus. Thus, the "moment of incarnation" is to be understood as functionally antecedent as it causes the "moment of faith."

In contrast to the several radical views that developed in the aftermath of the historical critical method, Kierkegaardian affinity to the orthodox Christian doctrine is noticeable in his emphasis on the eternal God who incarnated as the historical Jesus, simultaneously affirming the divinity and the humanity of Jesus. In spite of his emphasis on subjectivity, Kierkegaard does not even remotely infer that the disciples' acknowledgement of the divinity of Christ was a purely subjective projection of such a belief. Further, unlike the dialectical theologians who separate the historical Jesus and the Christ of faith, Kierkegaard is not embarrassed by the historicity and the problems surrounding it. Rather he would want to see it as an opportunity for faith, in that such an embarrassment could potentially generate offence—a necessary condition for truth.

If historical incarnation is pivotal in generating faith, why does Climacus reject historical inquiry as the basis of faith? How can Climacus exhibit an apparent indifference to historical evidence while maintaining that the historical presence of God is decisive for faith? Murray Rae points out that the term "'historical evidence' is misleading if not qualified." It is one thing to say that 'evidence' refers to coherence between one's beliefs and the historical life of Jesus, and quite another to say that historical evidence demonstrates the truth of one's beliefs. Climacus maintains only the former.

Climacus goes to the extent of arguing that a historical inquiry into the origins of Christianity "*can* be harmful for faith, indeed that it often is, but he does not suggest that it *must* be."[18] The problem is in confusing two views, which, according to Murray Rae, should be kept distinct.

16. PF, 14.
17. PF, 55.
18. Rae, "Kierkegaard and the Historians," 87.

The first is that "historical evidence cannot give rise to faith." The other is that "historical evidence is irrelevant to faith." Rae rightly observes that Climacus says only the former and not the latter. Climacus' position is that historical inquiry does not produce faith, but faith cannot be detached from history. Nantlais Williams, discussing the importance of the relation between Christian faith and history, says,

> Facts are essential for faith, but don't create it. "We *beheld* his glory," says John, not "We deducted it," nor "We had a strong feeling." It is the logic of the whole situation, not the logic of a syllogism that enables us to see a miracle in the mighty work. The deeds themselves led men to ask, "Who is this?" For the answer, those deeds had to be seen in the context of the words and the life of the one who performed them. It was not to leave men open-mouthed, but to open their eyes; the Christ came to the world.[19]

However, one's historical scholarship can indeed obstruct or even be harmful for the self when a misplaced accent is laid on the intellect to procure faith. The quantitative nature of historical inquiry, coupled with the human proclivity toward the self-deceptive dialectic between "knowing" and "willing" can easily lend itself to the detriment of the self, by causing an endless postponing of faith when "willing allows some time to elapse, an interim called: 'we shall look at it tomorrow.'"[20] Human reason can be instrumentalized, to the detriment of the self, in infinitely deferring faith for the future. However, as Rae rightly points out, Climacus' "target is the pretension that historical inquiry can displace the infinite passion of inwardness. Historical inquiry without such pretension might well be another matter."[21] The problem is in the presumption that human reasoning can procure truth. For Climacus, faith is not a work of human intellect; rather it is proper faith that leads to the right kind of reasoning by the intellect.

## On Whether Historical Knowledge Can Be the Basis for Faith

To get to the heart of Climacus' understanding, one has to answer how he reconciles holding to the centrality of historical incarnation for faith and his rejection of historical scholarship/inquiry as the basis for it. Climacus

---

19. Williams, *Faith Facts History Science*, 85.
20. SUD, 94.
21. Rae, "Kierkegaard and the Historians," 91.

raises a question that has engaged both the historian and the believer in the title page of *Philosophical Fragments*. "Can a historical point of departure be given for an eternal consciousness; how can such a point of departure be of more than historical interest; can an eternal happiness be built on historical knowledge?" In the introduction to the *Concluding Unscientific Postscript*, Climacus raises this question again and immediately clarifies his purpose. He writes, "In order, however, to avoid confusion, it should immediately be borne in mind that the issue is not about the truth of Christianity but about the individual's relation to Christianity, consequently not about the indifferent individual's systematic eagerness to arrange the truths of Christianity in paragraphs but rather about the concern of the infinitely interested individual with regard to his own relation to such a doctrine."[22]

The question before us therefore should be viewed in the light of the clarification that Climacus provides. Climacus is clearly not interested in raising a question about the truth of Christianity, which seems to be a positively settled issue at least for Kierkegaard. The issue of the truth of Christianity seems to be as good as it gets. Whether it is historical or archaeological data, there seems to be substantial evidence in support of the Christian claims. Likewise, an examination of the biblical manuscripts suggests an overwhelming accuracy in the preservation of the original texts, especially when compared to other manuscripts of such antiquity. So if one were to raise the question of the truth of Christianity and follow through with the available criteria of historical research, one could perhaps pronounce a verdict in its favor.

However, Climacus suggests that, in the final analysis, the question is not really about "the truth of Christianity" but about "the individual's relation to Christianity." More pointedly, he finds historical evidence insufficient as grounds for faith, where faith is understood not as "the truth of Christianity" but as "the individual's relation to Christianity." This distinction informs us as to why Climacus, while endorsing a philological undertaking, finds historical inquiry to be insufficient grounds for faith. Moreover, Climacus recognizes how an inquiry into the objective truth of Christianity can come in the way of one's subjective relation to such a doctrine, or better still, how the question of the truth of Christianity can function as a smokescreen for someone who does not want to have faith. Given that human rationality often takes the shape of the individual inquirer's will and affections, it is evident that it functions to protect self-interests

22. CUP, 15.

(especially where personal interests are involved), rather than as a neutral instrument to procure truth. Thus, Climacus argues that any claim to a disinterested inquiry as regards Christian faith is a contradiction, since personal interestedness influences one's response to Christ; where offence and faith are equal possibilities, an objective inquiry cannot become a vehicle to yield Christian faith.

Climacus finds more reasons as to why historical scholarship would fail to generate faith. First, it is in the nature of history that its content be unavailable for immediate perception. Since the "immediate sensation and immediate cognition cannot deceive,"[23] an illusiveness is introduced by the historical. Climacus thus locates one's focus on the objective truth of Christianity upon the self's movement from immediate cognition to objective knowledge—the transition from certitude to incertitude. Evans illustrates this Climacean point well. He writes, "Thus, when a person sees a star or experiences an event, *something* is immediately present and certain. However, as soon as the person forms a judgment about the content of the experience, for example, by holding the belief that the star is a *star*, an objective part of the physical world, then there is uncertainty, because the reality of the star as a public object with a history cannot be immediately sensed."[24]

Therefore, it seems as though the process of an immediate experience becoming one's knowledge would inadvertently bring about the problem of uncertainty, because on reflection the immediate becomes the past, and as Climacus says, "It is just as if reflection removed the star from his senses."[25] Likewise, if faith is Christianly understood as a relationship that acknowledges the Lordship of Christ, then for that very reason, it can be built only on an immediate Christ-encounter rather than on a cognitive reflection of the encounter. This entails that faith cannot be built on second-hand cognitive reflections of the Christian doctrines, except of course when such a reflection is accompanied by a personal Christ-encounter. Even an attempt to build one's faith on one's own past experience of Christ would be weak as faith demands a continual relationship with the absolute teacher. While there is an inherent certitude in our immediate experience, uncertainty commences when we reflect on it, with the possibilities of either being mistaken or being under an illusion about what was witnessed or encountered. The problem is further deepened in the case of past history, because our

23. PF, 81.
24. Evans, "Realism and Anti-Realism," 166. Cf. PF, 81.
25. PF, 81.

reflective consciousness is pressed into service upon that which was witnessed 2,000 years ago, with the potential for an ugly broad ditch between the first century events and the inquirer.[26]

Second, in a related sense, Climacus argues that the historical is contingent and thus shares a "non-necessary" character. Climacus categorizes all empirical occurrences—whether past, present, or future—as "historical," which "intrinsically has the *illusiveness* [*Svigagtighed*] of coming into existence."[27] They are historical because they have come into existence and, therefore, are not necessary, but contingent in nature. However, the past, having already occurred, may seem to appear necessary, especially as it now remains unchangeable and thus could prompt someone to consider it an unshakable ground for Christian faith. Detracting from this view, Climacus says, "The future has not occurred as yet, but it is not, *because of that*, less necessary than the past, inasmuch as the past did not become necessary by having occurred, but, on the contrary, by having occurred, it demonstrated that it was not necessary."[28] According to Climacus:

> Nature as spatial determination exists only immediately. Something that is dialectical with respect to time has an intrinsic duplexity [*Dobbelthed*], so that after having been present it can endure as a past. The distinctively historical is perpetually the past (it is gone; whether it was years or days ago makes no difference), and as something bygone it has actuality, for it is certain and trustworthy that it occurred. But that it occurred is, in turn, precisely its uncertainty, which will perpetually prevent the apprehension from taking the past as it had been that way from eternity.[29]

The contingent nature of historical occurrences stands in sharp contrast to the uncaused cause (God). To occur is to come into existence. But the necessary cannot come into existence because it "is always related to itself and is related to itself in the same way, it cannot be changed at all."[30] Time and again, thinkers, in trying to homogenize the historical with logical or metaphysical categories, have confounded the two presuming that the latter produced a higher kind of certainty. In any case, historicity brings with it a greater uncertainty than the logical or metaphysical, in that

---

26. I shall discuss Lessing's problem of the ugly broad ditch later in this chapter.
27. PF, 81.
28. PF, 77.
29. PF, 79.
30. PF, 74.

contingent occurrences are necessarily devoid of certitude similar to the conceptually demonstrable truths of reason. Epistemologically, this stance places Climacus in agreement with Lessing. If this is the nature of historical occurrences, how then can it be the basis for eternal happiness?

Third, Christian historical claims such as incarnation and resurrection are no ordinary historical occurrences, but have a unique feature in that they are based on an absurdity, that God became man. The central issue is that the eternal happiness of the individual "is decided in time through a relation to something historical that furthermore is historical in such a way that its composition includes that which according to its nature cannot become historical and consequently must become that by virtue of the absurd."[31] While it is the reality of this incarnation that distinguishes Christianity from pagan mythology and philosophy,[32] yet, for Climacus, "this historical fact which is the content of our hypotheses has a peculiar character, since it is not an ordinary historical fact, but a fact based on a self-contradiction."[33] So then, how can one historically prove the absurdity that God became man? According to Climacus, since a purely historical inquiry cannot yield a conclusion other than the historical, the impossibility of historical evidence resulting in faith cannot be construed either as the fault of the historian or that of history. For, even "if all the angels united, they would still be able to produce only an approximation, because in historical knowledge an approximation is the only certainty—but also too little on which to build an eternal happiness upon."[34]

Often a Christian, after beginning with this absurdity of God becoming man, restlessly attempts to prove other smaller historical details, presuming that he will in the end explain the absurdity. According to Climacus, the greatest absurdity "absorbs all the lesser" absurdities. He says, "The heart of the matter is the historical fact that the God has been in human form, and the other historical details are not even as important as they would be if the subject were a human being instead of the God. Lawyers say that a capital crime absorbs all the lesser crimes—so also with faith: its absurdity completely absorbs minor matters."[35] However, although incarnation is paradoxical and cannot be rationally explained, Climacus

---

31. CUP, 385.
32. Chapters 1 and 2 of CUP.
33. PF, 108.
34. CUP, 30.
35. PF, 103–104.

thinks that the assertion itself can be subject to rational examination. As Evans observes, "One cannot rationally understand the paradox, but one can hope to understand rationally why the paradox cannot be understood. In other words, the claim that reason has limits must itself be a claim that reason can adjudicate."[36]

The problem, therefore, is in confounding the distinction between a quantitative approach of historical research that leads to an approximation and a qualitative approach of faith that involves a personal and infinite interestedness in one's own eternal happiness.[37] Accordingly, the individual relates to eternal happiness only through uncertainty. When one tries to rid oneself of uncertainty to reach a higher quantitative certitude, one does "not have a believer in humility, in fear and trembling, but an esthetic coxcomb, a devil of a fellow who, figuratively speaking, wants to fraternize with God but, strictly speaking, does not relate himself to God at all."[38] Just as no one can make a lover doubt the blissfulness of love,[39] so also no one can steal eternal happiness from an individual who has faith. Doubt is not the nature of one who is in love or has faith. Like love, Climacus sees faith as passion, since it is a relationship with Christ. In the absence of faith, historical inquiry could very well take the inquirer away from the truth, since he is anyway devoid of the condition to receive it.

Conversely, in the lack of objective certitude, Climacus sees an opportunity for faith to enter, "for without risk, no faith; the more risk, the more faith."[40] According to Evans, "faith involves passion, and passion thrives on uncertainty, that risk is an essential element of faith."[41] To eliminate historical content from faith would be to eliminate the risk as well, which is detrimental for faith. Historical content then is pivotal for faith precisely because it introduces risk. Climacus therefore seems to maintain a careful balance in affirming empirical beliefs without establishing them on the basis of empirical evidence.

36. Evans, "Is Kierkegaard an Irrationalist?" 355.

37. CUP, 24, 89. This Climacean idea, as Evans suggests, may have led dialectical theologians like Tillich to propose faith as essentially independent of history. See Evans, "Empiricism, Rationalism and the Possibility," 147.

38. CUP, 455.

39. CUP. Climacus adds the footnote: "since erotic love is not the absolute *telos*, the comparison must be taken *cum grano salis* [with a grain of salt], all the more so because, in the sphere of esthetic, to be in love is outright bliss."

40. CUP, 209.

41. Evans, "Empiricism, Rationalism and the Possibility," 147–48.

*Historical Research and Its Sufficiency for Faith*

## Christian Witness and Historical Evidence

Climacus' emphasis of the "historical point of departure" as essential to the Christian faith automatically seems to bring with it a certain demand for objectivity, and yet he maintains a disregard for historical evidence. Scholarly discussions on the authenticity of the first century witnesses, as recorded by the evangelists inevitably raise questions in the mind of a believer. How do we know that the first century witnesses are true? Are the biblical accounts trustworthy? Is it possible that the disciples invented stories to emphasize the greatness of Jesus? These questions, however, are not merely intellectual ones, but are intertwined with one's passions and presuppositions. For a believer, there are several factors in history that makes a compelling case for faith. Thus, he not only draws from his faith but also reasons in the light of the available historical data.

Consider the case of resurrection. Some object to resurrection, arguing that Jesus was not really dead but only swooned on the cross and was resuscitated. Such suspicions could arise from a Humean type of presupposition that maintains an a priori rejection of resurrection. However, from the available historical data, a believer reasons that the Roman soldiers in charge of crucifixions, who were experts on their job, and especially, given that they could be executed for any negligence, would have ensured that Jesus was dead. Likewise, some have also suggested that the disciples may have deluded themselves into believing that Jesus was resurrected. However, given the nature of Christ's appearance after his death and the large numbers of witnesses to it, it is unlikely that resurrection is a belief that arose out of delusion. Another objection is that the disciples might have falsely spread the message that Jesus was resurrected. However, a believer naturally finds it more implausible that the disciples would risk their lives for a concocted story. A believer, therefore, not only functions purely on faith but also reasons with the available historical data to make sense of both his faith and the data.

Someone disinclined to believe the biblical witnesses, however, may reject both the belief and a believer's justification for it, on the basis that the evidence, which may be as good as it can get, is not sufficient to support the belief. He would thus justify his unbelief on the basis of a lack of an absolute certitude. Although a believer's justifications via historical inquiry seem to affirm his beliefs, they seem to be incapable of establishing faith in an unbeliever. This is not a case of unbiased reasoning leading to divergent beliefs; rather, it is a case of divergent beliefs leading to its corresponding justifications. That is, more than one's belief taking the shape of one's justification, it is one's justification that takes the shape of one's beliefs.

This perhaps explains Climacus' disregard for historical evidence. He writes, "Even if the contemporary generation had not left anything behind except these words, 'We have believed that in such and such a year the god appeared in the humble form of a servant, lived and taught among us, and then died'—this is more than enough."[42] "Enough for what?" asks Rae. He suggests two things for which it is not enough: "Firstly, it is not enough for one to live one's life as a disciple of Jesus. . . . Secondly, for the inquirer to decide whether or not the claim of faith is true."[43] Climacus would readily concur with Rae on the second point as the reason for rejecting an evidential basis for faith, for all along Climacus argues against any method that makes Christian faith merely probable. Where faith relies on a quantitative method of accumulation of evidence, the result is an approximation and faith is made probable. However, Climacus seems to claim precisely what Rae rejects, of the words being sufficient for one to live as a disciple. Climacus seems to affirm a basis for Christian faith that does not result in making faith probable. There is only one way to establish faith: a personal encounter with Jesus Christ.[44]

Climacean disregard for historical evidence seems to compromise the credibility of Christian faith. Had there been no record of the eyewitnesses, there would have been no possibility for faith; it would also be impossible to remain a believer if it were conclusively proven that the man called Jesus never existed or that he did not die and be resurrected. The historical record, then, is of utmost importance precisely because Christian faith has historical content. Neither Climacus nor Kierkegaard seem to define faith as a blind leap into the abyss, and neither have any doubts about the authenticity of the historical account—they treat the biblical record as reliable. Yet by holding that historical evidence is insignificant for faith, Climacus seems to argue against the necessity to examine the veracity of the historical content in Christian beliefs. This way, Climacus distinguishes between knowing historical content of Christian beliefs and establishing Christian faith on historical evidence. However, Climacus seems to allow enough evidence, just pertaining to minimal historical data, as necessary for Christian faith. That is, if there were clear historical evidence against the

42. PF, 104.
43. Rae, "Kierkegaard and the Historians," 92.
44. PF, 100–2.

historical claims of Christianity, or if the scrap of paper, which Climacus seems happy with the disciples leaving behind as evidence, were absent, then Climacus would readily concede. In this sense, Climacus makes faith vulnerable to historical data and is technically not against the principle of falsification.

Climacus' thoughts on the sufficiency of the early witnesses leaving nothing more than a scrap, would have to be understood in the background of his argument against a quantitative accumulation of historical evidence, which according to his calculus, carries no value in establishing faith. Here he remains consistent in claiming that faith is established only on the basis of a personal encounter with Christ. As Climacus says, "Only the person who personally receives the condition from the god (which completely corresponds to the requirement that one relinquish the understanding and on the other hand is the only authority that corresponds to faith), only that person believes."[45] Given this theological commitment of Climacus, all other factors, such as possessing sufficient historical evidence of what is believed, would only be incidental and not essential.

This however raises a problem: if a belief can be held without sufficient evidence (historical or rational), then what distinguishes a false belief from a true belief? Climacus does not suggest that one is free to hold any belief as true. While objectively historical inquiry can arbiter between a false belief and a true belief, and perhaps even conclude that Christian belief is true within the bounds of historical approximation, it still cannot establish faith. Rae distinguishes Kierkegaard, who argues that Jesus Christ is both the redeemer and the prototype, from Climacus, who is concerned only about how an individual becomes a Christian and is uninterested in the amount of historical evidence required to sustain the Christian faith. Rae argues that, for a follower, a prototypal role mandates reliable data about Jesus' life and character. According to Rae, Kierkegaard also "insists that Christian faith must be related to an objective ground. Without that objective ground, called 'an historical point of departure' by Climacus, the Socratic proposal for learning the Truth is victorious by default."[46] However, it is really hard to sustain the distinction that Rae holds between Kierkegaard and Climacus, on historical evidence. In fact, Kierkegaard seems to affirm the Climacean disregard for historical evidence as the basis for faith. Further, one could also maintain that a follower, who lives by faith, does not necessarily derive

---

45. PF, 103.
46. Rae, "Kierkegaard and the Historians," 93.

the historical data about the prototype [Christ] via historical inquiry, but rather by belief in the witnesses of the Scriptures through the enabling of the Spirit.

The question however is this: how is the inquirer to decide whether or not the claim of faith is true? The Kierkegaardian/Climacean position on this, as Rae rightly observes, "is that human beings are never in a position to judge the Truth. Rather, the appearance of God in time judges humanity, calls into question the criteria by which we presume to decide what is and is not possible for God, and requires that we relinquish our allegiance to the categories within which we have understood the world. This is the human decision and the only human contribution—to let go of the understanding. The individual does not also decide that the Truth is to be believed; that privilege comes as pure gift."[47] In other words, Climacus claims that the minute we employ a human theory of truth to test the claims of faith, human takes precedence over God, the temporal over the eternal. We become the judges, and God becomes the object of judgment, which for a believer cannot be the case. Rather, the incarnation of Jesus judges man in every situation.

Likewise, while Climacus sees the danger of critical scholarship in obstructing faith, he does not see the employment of the services of critical scholarship as justifying unbelief. With his typical irony, Climacus writes in the *Postscript*,

> So I assume . . . that the enemies have succeeded in demonstrating what they desire regarding the Scriptures, with a certainty surpassing the most vehement desire of the most spiteful enemy—what then? Has the enemy thereby abolished Christianity? Not at all. Has he harmed the believer? Not at all, not in the least. Has he won the right to exempt himself from the responsibility for not being a believer? Not at all. That is, because these books are not by these authors, are not authentic, are not *integri* [complete], are not inspired (this cannot be disproved, since it is an object of faith), it does not follow that these authors have not existed and, above all, that Christ has not existed.[48]

In the above passage, Climacus is confident about the existence of Christ and the reliability of biblical witnesses. He is unshaken by the vagaries of scholarly endeavor. For the same reason he would be opposed to

---

47. Ibid., 92.
48. CUP, 30.

the separation of the "Christ of faith" from the "Jesus of history," as it is a result of a warped mode of inquiry. Since Christian beliefs have definitive historical content, history is crucial; yet it stands not on critical scholarship but on faith. This however does not mean that historical critical scholarship cannot be of secondary use to faith, which has already been established on some other ground.

All that Climacus contends is that faith cannot be grounded in the evidencing process. Evans argues that the Climacean rejection of historical evidence is to prevent faith from becoming a subject of endless scholarly debate. Once we ground our faith in the evidencing process, the question would arise as to how much of one's historical research can be considered adequate for faith. Since it is no ordinary occurrence, and as eternal happiness is at stake, no amount of evidence would be sufficient for faith. Further, a Christian "does not have the luxury of waiting for the scholars to reach an agreement, which will never happen in any case,"[49] to conclude in the end that there is enough historical evidence for him to now become a believer. Yet, this does not logically force Climacus "to rule out historical evidence as a supplementary basis for faith, since it does not follow from the admission of such evidence that the decision to believe would thereby be indefinitely postponed."[50]

According to Evans, "it is possible for a believer to claim that it is significant that we have as much evidence as we have, and even to admit that some people would not find faith to be possible if they did not have evidence of reasonable, even if not decisive quality, while still properly believing that the decision is not, in the end, one which scholarship can settle."[51] He further suggests that it is the existence of faith that makes the question of evidence meaningful. In the absence of faith, there is no possibility for doubt either. Evidence, therefore, can play a significant role in "confirming an existing faith. From this perspective, faith makes it possible to appreciate and assess evidence in the proper light, thereby providing the believer with an assurance that his beliefs have not been undermined by various 'defeaters.'"[52] Since Christian faith is intricately connected to historical content, a believer is naturally concerned about historical accuracy. This value

---

49. Evans, *Kierkegaard: On Faith and the Self*, 160.
50. Emmanuel, *Kierkegaard and the Concept of Revelation*, 70.
51. Evans, *Kierkegaard: On Faith and the Self*, 161.
52. Emmanuel, *Kierkegaard and the Concept of Revelation*, 70. Also see Evans, *Kierkegaard: On Faith and the Self*, 161.

that Climacus attaches to the historical point of departure "leaves Climacus vulnerable to the falsification of religious beliefs by historical research."[53] Given this fact, both Evans and Rae ask, if the falsification of Christian beliefs were, in the least, a theoretical possibility, wouldn't believers need the assurance (emotive or intellectual) that that is not the case?

## The Use of "Evidence" in Faith Formation

Evans distinguishes between two kinds of probabilities: the objective and the subjective.[54] Objective probability is applicable in the cases of a repeatable situation, as in the outcome of the rolling of dice, where proportional results are predictable. Probability in a subjective sense applies to non-repeatable events, where there is a feeling of certainty. According to Evans, Climacus thinks that incarnation falls into the category of the "improbable" in the subjective sense, and since incarnation is historical for the believer, "he cannot believe that the objective probability of the event is low, since the objective probability of an event that has occurred is one."[55] For the believer, since incarnation is something that has already occurred, it is no longer improbable. Evans further believes that Climacus, even in his "hypothetical version of Christianity," does not imply that evidence is of no value whatsoever to the unbeliever, especially because faith is directly dependent on the reality of incarnation, which is the historical point of departure.

However, to the question "would an unbeliever involved in philological inquiry suddenly become a believer?" one could have a very different answer. Evans suggests that, if anything can be an occasion for a Christ-encounter, Climacus is then technically open to accepting that historical data as a possible mode through which Christ could encounter the individual. Despite Climacus' caution about the possible harm that historical inquiry can cause to faith, it technically can also provide an occasion for faith, even as the agent who causes faith is God rather than historical inquiry. In such a case, what is really significant is not so much the historical data but Christ, who encounters the individual, bringing about a conviction of sin and faith in the individual.

---

53. Rae, "Kierkegaard and the Historians," 91.
54. Evans, *Kierkegaard: On Faith and the Self*, 162.
55. Ibid., 164.

## Historical Research and Its Sufficiency for Faith

If historical data can at least provide an occasion, would the evidential apologist not be justified in presenting historical data as evidence? For Climacus, the problem would be in the presumption that evidence can provide faith to the unbeliever, where "evidence" is made to bear the weight of generating faith or at least to arbiter the case of faith. This presumption would nullify the absolute teacher as it relocates the possibility of availing truth within Socratic immanence. Climacus suggests that historical inquiry should not be stretched to deliver more than what is within its purview, for the historical data can never be "evidence" enough to produce faith.

However, can historical inquiry function to deliver corroborative evidence where faith is already present? While this is technically possible, the fact that one approaches the historical data as a believer and not as one who suspends faith during his historical inquiry, minimizes the value of such corroboration. Faith cannot be bracketed till a conclusion to the historical inquiry is reached, since eternal happiness is incommensurable with any quantitative approach. Climacus seems to think that any positive influence that historical data has on the believer, as in reinforcing one's belief in God, would be possible only as a continuation of Christ's encounter and not by the intrinsic value of the historical data. Such corroboration, in the end, only tends to prove one's lack of faith. He writes:

> Or there is a man, who says he has faith, but now he wants to make his faith clear to himself; he wants to understand himself in his faith. Now the comedy begins again. The object of faith becomes almost probable, it becomes as good as probable, it becomes probable, it becomes to a high degree and exceedingly probable. He has finished. . . . On the contrary, he has learned to know something different about faith than he believed and has learned to know that he no longer has faith.[56]

Evans questions whether the "subjective improbability of the paradox implies that the quality of the historical evidence is of no concern."[57] Of course, the quality of historical research is important. However, for Climacus, the research itself would not improve subjective improbability. What then should be made of a believer's psychological condition, where he feels better having found "evidence" for his faith? Such psychological pacification, for Climacus, functions no more than as a placebo. Addressing the

---

56. CUP, 211.
57. Evans, *Kierkegaard: On Faith and the Self*, 164.

question, "for whose sake is the proof/demonstration sought?" Climacus says:

> Here lies the difficulty, and I am again led back to learned theology. For whose sake is the demonstration conducted? Faith does not need it, indeed, must even consider it its enemy. When faith, however, begins to feel ashamed of itself, when, like a young woman in love who is not satisfied with loving but subtly feels ashamed of the beloved and consequently must have it substantiated that he is something exceptional, that is, when faith begins to lose passion, that is, when faith begins to cease to be faith, then the demonstration is made necessary in order to enjoy esteem from unbelief.[58]

It is possible that a believer's faith is threatened by historical scholarship. In such cases, Evans argues, there is, after all, room for historical research to substantiate what is believed/doubted. Yet, for Climacus, those doubts may be rooted in something more than an intellectual quest and may have to be addressed at a level that is more than mere scholarship. The unbelieving pseudonym's arguments for the inability of historical research to procure faith seem to anticipate Kierkegaard's belief in the role of the Holy Spirit in faith formation and its sustenance.

## Historicity and Contemporaneity

### Lessing's Problem: Historical Religious Knowledge as Not Self-Evident

Unlike the "Hegelian concept of the world-historical which supposes that the passing of time effects an inevitable improvement in our understanding, and thus makes certain what was not—or not readily—apparent in Christ's own time,"[59] Lessing thinks that the passing of time does the opposite, in that it is a movement away from the truth and the ugly broad ditch gets broader. "If I had lived at the time of Christ," argues Lessing, "then of course the prophecies fulfilled in his person would have made me pay great attention to him. If I had actually seen him do miracles . . . I would have believed him in all things in which equally indisputable experiences did not tell against him."[60] Here Lessing comes forth, argues Evans, as one "willing to

---

58. CUP, 30–31.
59. Rae, "The Forgetfulness of Historical-Talkative," 83.
60. Cited by Evans, "Empiricism, Rationalism, and the Possibility," 142. Cf. *Lessing's Theological Writings*, 51–52.

allow for the sake of argument that the historical evidence for Christianity is as good as can be imagined."[61] But later Lessing goes on to argue that the "contingent historical truths can never become a demonstration of eternal truths of reason, also that the transition whereby one will build an eternal truth on historical reports is a leap."[62] Here Lessing presumes that historical knowledge in principle can never be the basis for the eternal truth of religion. In so far as religious truths are eternal, Lessing finds it important to base them on reason, which, for him, has a greater universal appeal than contingent historical truths.

Evans rightly argues that Lessing's position, which considers historical knowledge as evidentially inadequate for religious knowledge, "obviously has a particular epistemological standard for religious knowledge," which requires of it "a level of certainty that historical knowledge cannot reach."[63] As far as Lessing's stance on historical religious knowledge or miracles is concerned, Climacus clarifies in the *Postscript* that "he [Lessing] does not deny (for he is quick to make concessions so that the categories can become clear) that what is said in the Scriptures about miracles and prophecies is as reliable as other historical reports, in fact, is as reliable as historical reports in general can be."[64] However, Lessing's primary problem is *historicity itself* because he considers historical beliefs as inferior to beliefs arising out of first-hand experience. Climacus also views that when our immediate perception recedes to reflection of what was perceived, its certainty is lowered to mere probability. However, unlike Climacus, for whom Christ rather than history is the basis of faith, for Lessing the problem of historicity becomes insurmountable, as he does not possess another means for Christian faith.

Against both Climacus and Lessing, it could be argued that the historical does not necessarily yield certitude inferior to first-hand experience.[65] Of some historical facts, say, the American Civil War or the assassination of Mahatma Gandhi, we have a certitude that is comparable to any first-hand experience. Sometimes, it is also possible to have genuine doubt about beliefs grounded in first-hand experience. In such a case, Evans argues, "the problem with historical religious beliefs lies not in their historical character

---

61. Evans, "Empiricism, Rationalism, and the Possibility," 142.
62. CUP, 93. Cf. *Lessing's Theological Writings*, 54–55.
63. Evans, "Empiricism, Rationalism, and the Possibility," 142–43.
64. CUP, 96.
65. Evans, "Empiricism, Rationalism, and the Possibility," 143.

but in their uncertainty, a characteristic of empirical beliefs in general, not simply historical ones."[66] One's objection to incorporate empirical content into faith may very well then be a rationalist objection to an empirical claim, rather than an empiricist objection. However, a rationalistic objection to an empirical claim is unjustifiable. Further, the rationalist's contention that "religious truths must be self-evident is itself far from self-evident."[67] Such rationalistic rejection of historical religious beliefs seems to impose upon religious truths a restriction that simply rules out any empirical content.

### Climacean Answer: Faith across the Ugly Broad Ditch

As a related concern, Lessing raises the problem of contemporaneity, giving expression to a general apprehension when he claimed that there was a greater likelihood of belief on his part had he been a contemporary of Jesus. For Lessing, the gap between the contemporary and the non-contemporary "is the ugly broad ditch that I cannot cross, however often and however earnestly I have tried to make the leap."[68] For Climacus however, Lessing's "broad ditch," based on whether one was historically contemporary with Christ or not, is an illusion. He says, "It is a leap, and this is the word that Lessing has employed within the accidental limitation that is characterized by an illusory distinction between contemporaneity and non-contemporaneity."[69] For Climacus, the contemporary follower is in no better position than the follower at second-hand, because "the contemporary follower, too, obtains a historical point of departure for his eternal consciousness, for he is indeed contemporary with historical event that does not intend to be a moment of occasion, and this historical event intends to interest him otherwise than merely historically, intends to be the condition for his eternal happiness."[70]

To both the contemporary follower and the follower at second-hand, it is the absolute paradox, the God-man/teacher, who provides the condition. The status of paradox itself does not change according to the learner's historical contemporaneity with the teacher—it still remains a paradox. A contemporary learner may be in a position to "acquire detailed historical

66. Ibid.
67. Ibid., 150.
68. CUP, 98. Cf. *Lessing's Theological Writings*, 55.
69. CUP, 98.
70. PF, 58.

information." However, with regard to the paradox which confronts him and his ascent to faith, he has nothing more at his disposal and is "in the very same situation as the follower at second-hand."[71] In contending that it was the historical contemporaneity that provided the condition, and not the paradox, Lessing aligns himself with the Socratic position, where "the learner is in possession of it; but if he is in possession of the condition, then he is *eo ipso* himself the truth, and the moment is only the moment of occasion."[72]

For Climacus, Lessing is simply mistaken, because, "knowing a historical fact—indeed, knowing all the historical facts with the trustworthiness of an eyewitness—by no means makes the eyewitness a follower, . . . because such knowledge means nothing more to him than the historical."[73] Climacus finds Lessing's claim that had he lived at the time of Christ, he would have believed him, as quite an unlikely possibility. Climacus spares him no kind words. He writes, "If someone coming later, someone who may even be carried away by his own infatuation, wishes to be a contemporary (in the sense of immediacy), he demonstrates that he is an impostor, recognizable, like the false Smerdis, by his having no ears—namely, the ears of faith—even though he may have the long donkey ears with which one, although listening as a contemporary (in the sense of immediacy), does not become contemporary."[74]

Lessing overlooked a crucial aspect in human nature when he connected faith only to contemporaneity. Becoming a follower not only involves the weight of the evidence presented to one's mind, but also the inclination of one's heart, apart from receiving the truth and condition from Christ. This understandably explains why not everyone who witnessed the miracles of Jesus believed in him. Therefore, if someone resists becoming a disciple by historically distancing himself from the event, he then deceitfully ascribes to contemporaneity (in the sense of immediacy) a status that is unwarranted, which then is used as a means of avoiding the truth. One should not be worried about such a person.[75]

---

71. PF, 59.
72. PF, 59.
73. PF, 59.
74. PF, 70.
75. PF, 70.

Truth and Subjectivity, Faith and History

## Every Disciple's Contemporaneity with Christ

Climacus argues, "The real contemporary is not that by virtue of immediate contemporaneity but by virtue of something else."[76] What is that "something else?" It is a personal knowledge that results from a personal encounter, when the teacher himself gives the condition.[77] Thus "the person who received the condition received it from the teacher himself, and consequently that teacher must know everyone who knows him, and the individual can know the teacher only by being himself known by the teacher."[78] Therefore, for Climacus, "Despite his being contemporary, a contemporary can be a noncontemporary; the genuine contemporary is the genuine contemporary not by virtue of immediate contemporaneity; ergo the noncontemporary (in the sense of immediacy) must be able to be a contemporary by way of something else by which a contemporary becomes a genuine contemporary. But the noncontemporary (in the sense of immediacy) is, of course, the one who comes later; consequently, someone who comes later must be able to be the genuine contemporary."[79]

In the *Postscript*, Climacus gives an additional insight into God's contemporaneity with a disciple. He argues that God being eternal is always contemporary to the existing individual because "His presence is an eternal contemporaneity."[80] Unlike the emperor who may not know his contemporary who knows him, God being eternal knows everyone who knows him. A ramification of this is that the God/teacher encounters the individual even in this present day. Climacus also says that the church, which is contemporary with the inquirer, provides an occasion for Christ to encounter the individual. Thereby equity is maintained for the learner of every generation in what is presented as "essentially Christian, since that is indeed what the church professes."[81] This would have remained more of an ideal in Kierkegaard's mind as the church of his own time was a poor representation of what was essentially Christian. Nevertheless, the best that the church can

---

76. PF, 67.

77. PF, 68.

78. PF, 68–69. Climacus' teacher-disciple analogy is parallel to the shepherd-sheep imagery of John 10:14—"I know my own and my own know me"—which points to a *personal knowledge* on the part of the teacher/shepherd, unlike the emperor who even if he knows (PF, 66–68), would only know that such and such was a soldier.

79. PF, 67.

80. CUP, 183.

81. CUP, 39.

provide is only an occasion for the learner, for it is ultimately God himself who gives the condition.

The Climacean thesis against Lessing's problem is that the *ugly broad ditch* was as ugly as it could be for the eyewitness as it was for Lessing, for the transition into faith is a qualitative leap and not a quantitative one. For Lessing, the ditch gets quantitatively outsized with the passage of time and he finds nothing to redress the aggravating problem. The Climacean alternative is that the individual of every generation believes "by virtue of the condition he himself receives from the god." The reports of both the first century eyewitness and today's church merely provide the occasion.[82] Therefore, Climacus argues, "if the one who comes later receives the condition from the god himself, then he is a contemporary, a genuine contemporary—which indeed only the believer is and which every believer is."[83] Every believer is a contemporary as he, through faith, believes that God is *Emmanuel—God with us*.[84]

Climacus defends the disciple's proximity to Christ by positing that a disciple is a contemporary of Christ by virtue of faith. In doing so, he argues not only against Lessing's criticism, but also against any system that divides the "Jesus of history" and the "Christ of faith." For Climacus, it is Christ who encounters the individual both in the first century and today. Kierkegaard, clarifying his view on this issue, elucidates in his *Journals*. He writes, "Contemporaneity or non-contemporaneity makes no essential difference; A historical point of departure (and this it is also for the contemporary, the historical, that God [*Guden*] exists [*er til*]—that is, exists by having come into the sphere of actuality [*bleven til*])—for an eternal decision is and remains a leap."[85] For Climacus therefore, a real contemporary "is not an eyewitness (in the sense of immediacy), but as a believer he is a contemporary in the *autopsy* of faith."[86] Many an argument could be supplied to explain concepts such as the incarnation, Trinity, miracles, and resurrection. However, there can be a real grasp of those concepts, only when one has faith as a prior condition.

---

82. PF, 104.
83. PF, 69.
84. Isa 7:14; Matt 1:23.
85. JP, 3: 2354.
86. PF, 70. Hong's translation carries the endnote: "literally, 'the personal act of seeing' (Greek: *autos*, self + *optos*, seen)"

## Conclusion

On Climacus maintaining that the historical event is decisive for faith there is little doubt, lesser still the contention that belief in Jesus as God must involve some true historical beliefs about Jesus. However, faith is not established on the basis of historical inquiry, but rather by "a transforming encounter with Christ, [which] is epistemically antecedent to particular historical beliefs about him."[87] In that case, it is possible that one believes in the historical record because of his faith in Jesus, rather than that he has faith in Jesus on the basis of the historical record. In a more general sense, one's view of historical religious beliefs seems to depend on the religious orientation of the individual. While it may be true that a believer, who begins with the possibility of miracles, may want to see a miracle even when there isn't one, yet if a miracle were to happen, he is nevertheless in a position to accept it. In contrast, an unbeliever who rejects a priori, the very possibility of miracles, would not experience a miracle, even if there was one.

A historical religious belief cannot directly result from purely historical analysis, as one can look at certain historical data meaningfully only as a believer. So Kierkegaard writes, "let miracle be what it is: an object of faith."[88] In the case of a believer, the reliability of historical records is accepted by virtue of its consistency with what the believer already knows by faith. Would this amount to special pleading for religious beliefs? Perhaps not, for any belief pertaining to sense perception follows the same steps— what is perceived is judged on the basis of what is already known on some other grounds, which in the case of a believer, is faith.

---

87. Rae, "Kierkegaard and the Historians," 90. This view is also held by Evans. See *Passionate Reason*, 156.

88. JP, 3: 2720.

# 6

# Kierkegaardian Insights for Christian Witness and Apologetics

*For whose sake is the demonstration conducted? Faith does not need it, indeed, must even consider it its enemy. — CUP, 30.*

*And he expounded the matter to them from morning till evening, testifying to the kingdom of God and trying to convince them about Jesus both from the Law of Moses and from the prophets. And some were convinced by what he said, while others disbelieved. — ACTS 28:23–24.*

## SECTION A

### Kierkegaard and Apologetics

ALTHOUGH KIERKEGAARD IS NOT a typical theologian, one can notice a clear invitation to Christian discipleship and imitation of Christ from the large corpus of his Christian discourses. His well-known critique of the Danish church of his time is really a call to practice a truer discipleship, one that goes beyond understanding Christian doctrines to personal appropriation and practice of faith. Similar to Paul's confession, "I have become all things to all men, that I might by all means save some,"[1] Kierkegaard delineates his authorial strategy of utilizing "everything to get as many as possible, everyone if possible, to accept Christianity—but then not to be so very scrupulous about whether what one got them to accept actually was Christianity. My strategy was: with the help of God to utilize everything to make clear what in truth Christianity's requirement is."[2]

One can also notice, although not overtly, that he engages in a type of apologetics that provides justification for Christian faith. Since it involves arguments that outline the limits of reason, it does not take the shape of apologetics, as it is practiced today. In fact, he might even come across as being anti-apologetics, given his use of indirect communication and his opposition to the rationalistic and evidential approaches to faith that apologetics has come to be associated with. However, recognition of the limits of human reasoning would in itself not disqualify him as a type of Christian apologist. Kierkegaard declares his opposition to a particular type of apologetics in *Sickness Unto Death*: "it is certain and true that the first one to come up with the idea of defending Christianity in Christendom is de facto a Judas No. 2: he, too, betrays with a kiss, except that his treason is the treason of stupidity. To defend something is always to disparage it."[3] According to Sands, this position of Kierkegaard "is repudiating, not a defense of *true* Christian faith, but a defense that is *untrue to* the Christian faith."[4] After all, in *The Point of View*, he clarifies: "I have never broken with Christianity or given it up; to attack it has never entered my mind. No, from the time it was possible to speak of the application of my powers, I had firmly resolved to employ everything to defend it, or in any case to present it in its true form, because, through my upbringing, I very early was already able to ascertain how seldom Christianity is presented in its true form, how those who defend it most often betray it."[5]

Thus, although a strange one, this self-acknowledged task of defending Christianity turns Kierkegaard into a type of apologist within Christendom. Climacus argues that it is more difficult to introduce true Christianity within Christendom, which holds onto a "form of religion."[6]

1. 1 Cor 9:22.
2. PV, 16.
3. SUD, 87.
4. Sands, *The Justification of Religious Faith*, 31.
5. PV, 80.
6. 2 Tim 3:5.

Within a Christian culture, one encounters cultural expressions that mimic Christian practices, which often makes it difficult to distinguish between genuine Christian faith and a form of religion. Thus he writes,

> The difficulty is much greater because this must and should occur quietly within the individual without any decisive external action. . . . If I am not a Christian, and the decision is to become a Christian, then Christianity helps me to become aware of the decision, and the distance between us helps just as the running start helps the jumper. But if the decision seems to have been made already, if I am already a Christian (that is, am baptized, which is still only a possibility), then there is nothing to help me become properly aware of the decision; but on the other hand there is something (which is the increased difficulty) that hinders me in becoming aware of it—namely, the semblance of a decision.[7]

The delusion within Christendom requires a unique strategy, as Kierkegaard points out in *The Point of View*: "If it is true that there actually are so few true Christians in Christendom, then these are *eo ipso* [precisely thereby] obliged to be missionaries, even though a missionary in Christendom will always look different from a missionary in paganism."[8] To the one deceived within Christendom, an apologist will have to employ a counter-deception and "the method must become indirect. In the communication of Christianity, when the situation is Christendom, there is not a direct relation, there is first of all a delusion to remove. The entire old science of arms, all the apologetics and everything belonging to it, serves instead, to put it bluntly, to betray the cause of Christianity."[9]

Climacus polemic against both pagan thought, which locates truth within the individual, and a Christian thinking that privileges human reason over revelation, are essentially aimed at Christendom. Following the recognition of Socrates as the best of the pagan philosophers, Climacus carries out an extensive defense of the superiority of Christ over Socrates and of Christianity over the Socratic conception of truth. In doing so, Climacus presents Christianity as better than other philosophical and religious systems. Likewise, his critique of the rationalistic approaches of Lessing and Hegel was primarily against their philosophized and cultural forms of religion, which elevated human reason over revelation.

---

7. CUP, 365–66.
8. PV, 47.
9. PV, 52–53.

However, Kierkegaard suggests that the moment of incarnation, or the Christ-encounter, necessarily leads an individual to one of two potential responses: faith or offence. Both of these, understandably, may come in varying forms. While genuine faith is characterized by imitation, love, and martyrdom, everything that replaces the authentic commitment of discipleship with various counterfeits—mere form of religion, scaffoldings of rational discourses, philosophical justifications, etc.,—are merely forms of offence. Although, Kierkegaard's target is not philosophy or rationality *per se*, yet he sees them as potential smokescreens that help dodge authentic Christian discipleship.

The unparalleled significance of the moment is such that it is the most pivotal point in history and impacts all of history. It also impacts the history of ideas—every philosophical idea since that moment, including the numerous philosophies that have circumvented Christian discipleship, is nonetheless affected by the Christian message. Apart from the dialectic across the secular and Christian divide of the West, both the *ad intra* and *ad extra* critiques of the various sins of commission and omission of the Church—the bitter wars of Crusades, slavery, etc.,—are made possible by the moment and its influence, especially by the Sermon on the Mount.

## Apologetics after Kierkegaard

With the rise of modern historicism as a sibling of modern science, it was assumed that the historical data that was available could serve as evidence for faith. On the one hand, historical data makes possible a rejection of the Christian message via the services of modern historicism, and on the other, it allows an over-enthusiastic use of evidential apologetics to establish faith. Both the polarities tend to use that which historical data cannot prove. Sharing the optimism of the Enlightenment led many a Christian thinker to harness modernistic approaches to arrive at objectivity in historical inquiry. While it must be granted that a believer could have his faith shaken or that an unbeliever could potentially become more sympathetic to Christian claims on account of historical research, more often it so happens that the pre-theoretical commitments of both the believer and the unbeliever influence the way the historical data is viewed. In other words, while historical research can be pursued with an unbiased scrutiny, the difficulty is in making the leap from knowing historical data to a trust in Christ. For a believer, while historical research may reinforce the case for Christian faith; for an unbeliever, it could serve to justify his rejection of the Christian faith.

The optimistic tone of the Enlightenment has been espoused by many an apologist of various religious and atheistic persuasions. Christian thinkers who were married to the modernistic outlook undertook the task of proving the existence of God or providing evidential proofs for the deity of Christ as objectively demonstrable. In his work, *Christian Apologetics*, Norman Geisler elaborates that Christian apologetics "is interested in defending the truths that Christ is the Son of God and the Bible is the word of God. However, prior to establishing these two pillars on which the uniqueness of Christianity is built, one must establish the existence of God . . ."[10] Geisler makes no reservations about his optimism when he writes, "It is the contention of this work (in part three) that evangelical Christian theism qualifies as the most systematically coherent theistic view on all three tests; consistency, empirical adequacy, and experiential relevance."[11] While a believer would readily grant that Geisler's claim is true, the question is whether faith is a prerequisite for such a conclusion. If it were, then according to Climacus, one would be arguing *from* a conclusion rather than *towards* it.

Earlier, William Paley had argued that if a person accidentally found a watch and a stone lying side by side in a field, he could conclude that the stone had always been lying there and, from the watch, that there existed a watchmaker. The watch indicates an intelligent purpose and inherent order. Similarly, the world displays an intelligent purpose and an inherent order, like a cosmic watch, which points to the cosmic watchmaker or God. While it may be granted that Paley's teleological argument makes perfect sense to a believer, Hume, contrary to Paley, argued that the apparent "design" could merely be a "happy accident," for theoretically it is possible that, given enough time, chance could have produced the order of nature.[12]

Paley and Hume cannot both be right. But, how is it that Paley and Hume argue toward opposing conclusions? For Kierkegaard, following Pauline assumptions, Paley and Hume argue from different vantage points—Paley, from a spiritually enlightened position and Hume, from a fallen natural man's position. A believer, whose spiritual eyes have been opened, arrives at his conclusion on account of the revelation he has received, which

---

10. Geisler, *Christian Apologetics*, 8–9.
11. Ibid., 147.
12. Hume, *Dialogues concerning Natural Religion*, pt. VIII.

may be called the "eyes of faith" or the "condition," without which he could also have been in Hume's position. Similarly, while a believer finds it outrageous to reason that time and chance could create a watch, a naturalist is equally outraged by the argument from design. Both the believer and the naturalist are convinced that their own argument is the most probable one. A pivotal question that an apologist should then ask is whether the evidential approach, which views external evidence in conjunction with certain tests for truth as sufficient to determine a given truth-claim, really works. Can the argument that attempts to evidentially prove the truth of theism, or further still, the divinity of Jesus, convince an unbeliever?

Climacus, in both *Fragments* and *Postscript*, argues that while Christianity may be all that it claims to be, an evidential approach cannot by itself cause faith in an individual. His claim is not that there is no value whatsoever in the objective demonstration of biblical truths, but rather that it is not sufficient to make someone a believer. While historical inquiry could be useful in answering legitimate questions and even perhaps in whetting the intellectual appetite of a believer, they hardly provide definitive and conclusive answers to an unbeliever. When evidential proofs are presented with the hope of convincing an unbeliever, an apologist overestimates the potential of the evidential approach. Such an approach fails to see some key factors that Kierkegaard takes for granted: a) sin and the self-deceptive nature of human soul entails that the fallen mind cannot grasp truths about God and self unless it is transformed; b) no knowledge of truth is possible via Socratic mediation as truth is revealed entirely by God/the moment of incarnation; c) Since (a) and (b), any human endeavor that pretends to transform the mind is a relapse into the Socratic Method; d) while the Socratic Method was valid outside Christ's revelation, reverting to it after the moment of incarnation is a subversion of the Christian message; e) and thus, "to approach Jesus Christ by means of what is known about him from history"[13] would be "blasphemy" as it indirectly reverts to the Socratic mode, since it still locates truth within historical research.

Often an apologist could attribute an instance of unbelief to the adamant disposition of the unbeliever (which may very well be the case!) rather than the possible ineffectiveness of the evidential approach itself. The oft-quoted biblical passage, "Ever since the creation of the world his invisible nature, namely, his eternal power and deity, has been clearly *perceived* in

---

13. PC, 29.

## Kierkegaardian Insights for Christian Witness and Apologetics

the things that have been made. So they are without excuse,"[14] is used to lay the entire burden of unbelief upon unbelievers, who do not believe despite the seemingly solid logical evidence. Rather, it would be important to know whether the above passage talks about an individual believing on the basis of the apologist's logical demonstration of truth or about a more direct kind of evidence that is perceptual in nature. As Kelly James Clark rightly asks, "The crucial question is how knowledge of God is communicated through these phenomena. Does this text indicate that knowledge of God is communicated *directly* or *via an argument*?"[15] In this case, it may be profitable for the apologist to recognize the connection between belief and perception rather than belief and rational argumentation.

Kierkegaard's assumption that a Christ-encounter necessarily leads to either faith or offence, is essentially Pauline. Paul argues that the gospel is a scandal and an offence to human reason—a stumbling block to the Jews and foolishness to the Greeks[16]—and rather than remove it, he made every effort to retain the scandalous nature of the gospel.[17] Yet, it is tempting for the apologist committed to enlightenment thinking, to use the midwifery assistance of reason to issue faith. In the process the original labels of the gospel as "paradoxical," or "scandalous," or "foolish," are replaced with "reasonable" and "logical." However, it is the spirit of Enlightenment that seeks to transform a belief that is foolish and scandalous into a rational belief. While the Pauline argument clearly preserves the "scandalous" and "foolish" tag of the gospel for those who are not spiritually regenerated, it is precisely faith, as a prior commitment, that makes the gospel reasonable for a believer. While the nature of Christian beliefs requires that the content of faith corresponds to facts and human reason, a believer's acceptance of the authority of the gospel itself is not a result of its correspondence to facts and the standards of human reason, but is rather a work of the Holy Spirit. As Raschke argues, "It is not without reason that Luther made the repeated argument that only the Holy Spirit can unveil the import of the text. Without the Spirit the mind is blinkered. Reformation theology, therefore, refutes the 'correspondence theory' of truth. . . . There can be no 'correspondence' at the scriptural level between word and thing unless

---

14. Rom 1:20. Emphasis added.
15. Clark, *Return to Reason*, 49.
16. 1 Cor 1:23.
17. Gal 5:11.

the 'thing' is transparently glimpsed from the perspective of one who has received grace through faith."[18]

A redefining of the gospel as rational with the view of making it more acceptable for the rationalist would alter the very nature of the gospel. It entails a reduction, where the gospel is reduced to propositional truths, where logic and semantics play the determining role at the expense of the miraculous and transformative power of the gospel. Although the supernatural and miraculous may be theoretically granted as possible, practically it finds no place within the cognitive landscape of "reasonable" gospel. However, if Christ causes faith, then it is entirely miraculous in nature. It may be argued that the ideal candidate on whom reason and logic should have been effective would have been the learned Saul. However, Saul's conversion, that resulted from his Christ-encounter, turns out to be a perceptual encounter rather than via a rationally demonstrated argument. As Raschke rightly argues,

> The theme of subjective truth, properly understood, has been far more congenial to the expansion of the gospel throughout the ages than any canon of propositional certitude. When evangelical believers undergo conversion by responding to an altar call and offer their own lives to Christ in a personal profession of faith, it is rarely the result of anyone having convinced them through careful and flawless reasoning that Jesus is their savior. It is usually because God ministering as the Holy Spirit has grappled with them in their private depths of confusion and doubt and given them a whole new inner lease of life. Paul may have convinced a few Athenian citizens that the "unknown God" they were worshiping was in fact the living creator. But Paul himself was not drawn to Christianity because some philosopher offered a better argument than the Stoics, Cynics, or Epicureans of his time. Saul of Tarsus became Paul the apostle because the resurrected Lord encountered him on the road to Damascus, said only a few soul-wrenching words to him, and left him speechless and dumbstruck.[19]

Expectedly, Kierkegaard's departure from modernistic and evidential apologetics has not been generously welcomed among Christian thinkers. The reasons are not too far-fetched to trace. Kierkegaard's thinking, for many a Christian apologist, axed the very branch on which they were positioned. Gordon H. Clark's evaluation of Kierkegaard reveals such

18. Raschke, *The Next Reformation*, 127.
19. Ibid., 19.

displeasure, when he writes, "the emphasis on subjectivity and the corresponding disparagement of objectivity results in the destruction of Christianity's objective historicity."[20] However, a closer reading of Kierkegaard shows that while he is committed to objective historicity, he places the weight of belief not on the objectivity of Christianity but on a personal encounter with Christ. Conversely, any attempt to base Christian faith upon objectivity would essentially undo the very essence of Christianity. Thus, in the *Book on Adler*, he writes, "If one were to describe this entire orthodox apologetic endeavor in a single sentence, yet also categorically, one would have to say: Its aim is to make Christianity probable. Then one must add: If this succeeds, then this endeavor would have the ironical fate that on the very day of victory it would have forfeited everything and completely cashiered Christianity."[21]

## Epistemic Status of Faith as Properly Basic

C. Stephen Evans argues that Climacus "sees faith as epistemologically basic, in something like Alvin Plantinga's sense of the term."[22] A basic belief is a belief that is not dependent on any other belief(s) or inference or argument. Plantinga argues for the possibility of holding certain basic beliefs without any breach to one's reasoning. According to him, religious beliefs are basic and fundamental in nature. They are beliefs that are not inferred or arrived at; rather, they are beliefs that are argued from. They are beliefs that are held without any evidential support from some other beliefs. Yet, while a basic belief is not based on any other belief, it could be the basis for other beliefs. Such a system of beliefs, for Plantinga, forms the human noetic structure.[23]

Basic beliefs could be a result of one's perception. For example, my belief that this is a red car is acquired immediately and not on the basis or support of any other belief. In rare cases, if I am color blind or if I am suffering from a jaundiced eye, it is possible that I am wrong in my perception. The question, however, is not which belief is true, but how is one's belief obtained and sustained. Typically, perceptual beliefs are held without the

---

20. Clark, "A Christian Appraisal of Contemporary Philosophy," 5.
21. BA, 39.
22. Evans, "The Relevance of Historical Evidence," 475. Cf. Plantinga, "Reason and Belief in God."
23. Plantinga, "Reason and Belief in God," 48.

support of other beliefs. My belief that the sun rose this morning is a basic belief. However, when I infer that I perceive the sun rising because of the earth's rotation on its axis around the sun, I have inferred it on the basis of other beliefs, and hence it is a non-basic belief. So there are beliefs that are non-basic, which are beliefs that are inferred or held by the evidential support of other beliefs. Basic beliefs could also be acquired through testimony. One simply believes that the British ruled India for more than 300 years, or that Mahatma Gandhi was assassinated, when a teacher so instructs or by believing what one reads in a book. For instance, as Plantinga argues, our belief in other minds is basic. Unless one is predisposed to skepticism, a person normally reasons *from* the belief that there are other minds. Plantinga argues that our belief in God is similar to our belief in the existence of other minds. He writes, "Of course there may be other reasons for supposing that although rational belief in other minds does not require an answer to the epistemological question, rational belief in the existence of God does. But it is certainly hard to see what these reasons might be. Hence my tentative conclusion: if my belief in other minds is rational, so is my belief in God. But obviously the former is rational; so, therefore, is the latter."[24]

Likewise, Evans argues "Climacus thinks that Christian faith is not only basic, but properly basic for the believer."[25] For Climacus, faith is established by God's encounter with the individual when both "faith" and the "condition" for faith are given. The individual does not normally scrutinize the truth about historicity, although there may be some researcher who would be interested in scrutinizing the claims through a thorough study. It is perfectly possible that one simply believes a testimony about Jesus on listening to a sermon or reading a book. In the case of the one who is keen on solid evidence based in the first century, historical data could provide an occasion for encountering the truth, but again only as an act of God. Thus Climacus says in *Fragments*, "By *means of* the contemporary's report (the occasion), the person who comes later believes by virtue of the condition he himself receives from the god."[26] Climacus therefore sees faith as epistemologically basic and hence as antecedent to one's historical religious beliefs.

An important question to consider is, "why didn't everyone who encountered the same historical events of the first century believe in Jesus?" Some followed but others took offence. Those who took offence also

---

24. Plantinga, *God and Other Minds*, 271.
25. Evans, "The Relevance of Historical Evidence," 475.
26. PF, 104.

witnessed his miracles and saw that he cast out demons. However, having already rejected his authority, they interpreted his miracles as possible as a result of being possessed by the "prince of demons."[27] In this case, an a priori acceptance or rejection of his authority seems to have determined how his miracles were interpreted. Therefore, faith functioning as a basic belief can bring about acceptance of particular historical details associated with one's faith, and likewise, one's a priori rejection of faith can entail rejection of historical details associated with the faith. Either ways, a Christ-encounter can bring about opposing responses—some towards surrender and some to antagonism.[28]

## Spirit Gives Life to the spirit: Kierkegaard's Pneumatological Understanding

Undoubtedly, the entire Kierkegaardian corpus of texts is christological in focus and, despite Climacus' confessed position as an unbeliever, his inquiry is still confined to Christology, which recognizes a) the unavoidability of a paradox in God becoming man, and b) how the incarnation of Christ is the most crucial point in faith formation. Although this christological preoccupation of Kierkegaard seems legitimate given the immediate concerns he raises, one may notice the absence of a properly trinitarian explication of God. Yet the purview of his pneumatological understanding, which appears as a small section in *For Self-Examination*, permeates his entire corpus, particularly his Christology, in that it is assumed that the moment of incarnation is transformed into the moment of faith only by the work of the Holy Spirit. Kierkegaard acknowledges the creative and preservative activity of the Holy Spirit as He "who gives life" and thus gives faith, hope, and love.[29]

Central to Kierkegaard's departure from the Hegelian vision is the thinking about God and this departure is noticeable not only in his Christology, but also in his Pneumatology. Hegel's quasi-pantheistic view of trinity, as Kärkkäinen explains, is, "The Essential Being, pure abstract being, resembles the role of the 'Father.' The Explicit Self-Existence refers to the entrance of the abstract Spirit into existence through the creation of the

---

27. Cf. Mark 3:22.
28. CUP, 215.
29. See the section "It is the Spirit," in FSE, 73–87.

world ('Son'). God moves outside himself, entering into relationship with that which is other than himself. The Self-Knowledge is the Spirit passing into self-consciousness."[30] Corresponding to Hegel's vision of God is his vision of humanity. He sees Christ as the person in whom "the infinite Spirit (God) and the finite spirit (human being) are brought together. However, unlike most of his predecessors, these two are not radically different or mutually incompatible."[31] Unlike Hegel, Climacus argues that they are mutually incompatible and thus categorizes the God-man as the "absolute paradox." God as the totally other, different from everything created, is what makes incarnation a paradox, which in the Kierkegaardian thinking is neither reconciled nor cancelled.

Kierkegaard understands human being as a spirit. He writes, "A human being is spirit. But what is spirit? Spirit is the self. But what is the self? The self is a relation that relates itself to itself or is the relation's relating itself to itself in the relation; the self is not the relation but is the relation's relating itself to itself."[32] A parallel is noticeable between the Augustinian explication of the Spirit and its function as the bond of love and the Anti-Climacean connection between human self as spirit and its relationality. Kierkegaard alludes to Augustine's *De Trinitate*, which attributes "love" specifically to the Holy Spirit within his trinitarian theology. In his *De Fide Et Symbolo*, Augustine states that "The Holy Spirit is the communion of Godhead, the mutual affection and love of Father and Son."[33]

Explaining Augustine's relational character of the Spirit, McIntyre writes, "He finds in Scripture the mutual love of Father and Son . . . and on the other hand has fully described the work of the Spirit *ad extra* in enabling believers to dwell in the love of God; he then identifies the Spirit, as known in his work with believers, with the love which is internal to the Godhead, is itself eternal and bonds Father and Son together."[34] Following the doctrine of appropriations, the Augustinian view of Trinity identifies the Holy Spirit with the communion or love within the Godhead. A parallel to Augustine's understanding of the Holy Spirit and what it implies to human relations is reflected in Kierkegaard's notion of the human spirit as

---

30. Kärkkäinen, *Pneumatology*, 60.

31. Ibid., 60.

32. SUD, 13.

33. Augustine, *De Fide Et Symbolo*, 9.19. Cited by McIntyre, *The Shape of Pneumatology*, 145.

34. McIntyre, *The Shape of Pneumatology*, 147.

"a relation that relates itself to itself," as a form of communion or a relation of love. Just as much as humanity is defined in the light of Christ, the prototype, human spirit is seen in the light of the Holy Spirit, as a relation. Thus, he writes of the early disciples, "by loving God, in order that they might continue in love, they joined with God, so to speak, in loving this unloving world—the life-giving Spirit brought them love. Thus the apostles, in conformity with their prototype, resolved to love, to suffer, to endure all things, to be sacrificed in order to save this unloving world. And this is love."[35] Undoubtedly, the prototype that Kierkegaard refers to is Christ, yet only as an interpenetration[36] of the second and third persons of the Trinity.

Kierkegaard's Christology and Pneumatology are interdependent and mutually enriching. In unearthing Kierkegaard's insights for apologetics today, we ought to understand Kierkegaard's Pneumatology, that primarily credits the Spirit as the giver of faith, hope, and love, and as the one who makes both the Christ-encounter and Christ-imitation possible. It is through his pneumatological underpinnings, which define the human being as spirit, that Kierkegaard accredits the human possibility not only to relate to the transcendental but also to the possibility of receiving divine revelation. Thus he writes, "No, the Spirit comes—and brings the gifts of the spirit, life and spirit. The Spirit brings faith, the faith—that is, faith in the strictest sense of the word, this gift of the Holy Spirit—only after death has come in between."[37]

The life that the Spirit grants in Kierkegaard's pneumatological thinking emphasizes a discontinuity between "natural life" and "new life," which echoes the Pauline accent on the break that Christ brings about with one's previous life.[38] This involves a dying to the world and to the self;[39] and the Spirit transforms the old into an ontologically new self. Kierkegaard's pneumatological explorations are purely within the scope of Christology, which explains why his section called, "It Is the Spirit" follows immediately after "Christ Is the Way" in *For Self-Examination*. The work of the Holy Spirit is

---

35. FSE, 85.

36. *Perichoresis* (interpenetration) is a doctrine that was explicated by early church fathers, which is renewed in the works of contemporary theologians like Miroslav Volf and John Zizioulas.

37. FSE, 81.

38. FSE, 76. Cf. 2 Cor 5:17 "Therefore, if anyone is in Christ, he is a new creation; the old has passed away, behold, the new has come."

39. FSE, 77.

then not merely to make possible a better life in general but to give a new life—one that comes following death to self and the world. Thus he writes, "It is when all confidence in yourself or in human support, and also in God in an immediate way, is extinct, when every probability is extinct, when it is dark as on a dark night—it is indeed death we are describing—then comes the life-giving Spirit and brings faith. This faith is stronger than the whole world; it has the power of eternity; it is the Spirit's gift from God, it is your victory over the world in which you more than conquer."[40]

Kierkegaard's Pneumatology, where faith, hope, and love are entirely given by the Spirit to a believer as part and parcel of the new life in Christ, better explains Climacus' discourse on how truth and the condition for truth are procured. Such a miraculous bestowal of the new life by the Spirit endows the believer with a capacity for faith that is not accessible within the former self or natural human reasoning. Climacus' opposition to human reason or historical evidence functioning as a vehicle for truth/faith is precisely in that such an approach fails to see the discontinuity of a life of faith from the former self. It could also be concluded that the Climacean alternative to the Socratic Method for procuring truth anticipates the person and work of the Holy Spirit in Kierkegaard's Christian writings.

While the full extent of the pouring of the Holy Spirit in the Pentecost comes after Christ's ascension, the inverse order may be seen in an individual actually coming to faith, in that a proper understanding of Christ follows the work of the Holy Spirit. Given this structure, it becomes pivotal to locate Kierkegaard's Pneumatology within his robust Christology. What the contemporary Eastern Orthodox theologian, John Zizioulas, contends as being the role of the Holy Spirit best informs the Kierkegaardian view on the subject. Zizioulas writes, "The Holy Spirit is not one who *aids* us in bridging the distance between Christ and ourselves, but he is the person of the Trinity who actually realizes in history that which we call Christ. . . . In this case, our Christology is *essentially* conditioned by pneumatology, not just secondarily as in the first case; in fact it is *constituted* pneumatologically."[41]

---

40. FSE, 82.
41. Zizioulas, *Being as Communion*, 110–11.

## SECTION B

## Hindu Sense of History and Christian Apologetics

The moment of incarnation as conceived by Kierkegaard is unique and of the utmost significance for human salvation. However, how does the moment of incarnation feature within the Hindu context, which seems to adopt a sense of time/history, which by its nature cannot ascribe such significance to that moment? In this section, I shall look at the Hindu sense of history and some hurdles it raises for the appropriation of the historical Jesus and what it implies for Christian apologetics in a Hindu setting. Given his acknowledged undertaking was more as a "missionary in Christendom," invoking Kierkegaard for a discussion on the Hindu sense of history and apologetics may seem inappropriate. Nonetheless, I believe Kierkegaard's insights are useful. Further, my own awareness to the issue of faith and history as an Indian Christian trying to negotiate between the two was primarily accentuated through a reading of Kierkegaard. Also, Kierkegaard's rejection of a modernistic approach to history makes his approach accessible for this context.

It is possible that the rigor associated with historical inquiry within the Western civilization is, to some extent, a result of the Christian faith where Christians had to constantly appeal to the historical nature of their faith. Contrastingly, in the religious faiths of the East, as in the case of Hinduism, which never appealed to historical verification as regards its religious beliefs, a corresponding disregard for historical inquiry and the rigors associated with it is noticeable. As A. G. Hogg identifies, "a very important reason why the historical element is not still more fundamental in Hindu religion is simply the absence from Indian history of a sufficiently tragic and universally inspiring figure."[42] The semblance between historical analysis and empirical research could also have influenced the general attitude to all empirical inquiry in the West, making possible the enormous scientific progress.

### The Sense of History in Traditional Indian Thought

A unique feature of the Hindu civilization is that the entire religious narrative employs a cyclical sense of time, where the narrative is relegated to

42. Hogg, *Karma and Redemption*, 8.

an ahistorical/mythical realm. This shields the Hindu religious beliefs from problems surrounding the historicity of their beliefs. "Myths" often refers to a grand metanarrative that gives meaning to particular narratives, and as meaning-givers, they are an essential part of every religious narrative. The accent here is not on their verifiability, as myths by definition are set outside the purview of historical verification. However, "myths" also refers to something imagined and unreal, when contrasted with that which is real or historical. The distinction between myth and history has led to a long tradition of rigorous historical inquiry in the Christian West and a lack thereof in the Hindu context.[43] In Hinduism, where religious beliefs are not connected with history, critical inquiry has given rise to rigor in its speculative philosophy, where the emphasis is on the coherence of thought rather than correspondence to facts.[44] The association of historical rigor with Christian beliefs is often met with genuine indifference in the Indian context, including within a Christian environment.

Romila Thapar in *Time as a Metaphor of History* elucidates the Hindu view of time/history as cyclical. The Hindu cyclical view of history holds time as an eternally stable entity in which all of nature is in an endless cycle of births, deaths, and rebirths. Our present human history is seen as just a part of that grand cycle. Adherence to such a view of time, although it does not imply a rejection of human history *per se*, cannot attach significance to it. The time that is at our disposal becomes a small and insignificant part of an unending cycle. Quoting Mircea Eliade, a historian of religion, Thapar notes that in the Hindu understanding of time, there is "an eternal cyclic repetition of time, so huge in concept that human activities become miniscule and insignificant in comparison. Cyclic time is continuous, without a beginning or an end."[45]

Most importantly, this view assigns a diminutive role to the individual, as he believes that his contribution in life is also insignificant. Further, one is not running against time when eternity is at one's disposal. The argument

---

43. The issue, though essentially a socio-religious one, also has economic implications. The patents for parts of Indian traditional knowledge practiced for centuries have been lost to multinational Western companies simply because there were no written records of them. Notable among these are the medical utility of Neem and the unique qualities of Basmati rice. Only a proper record of traditional knowledge can prevent Indian users from having to pay Western companies, to access their own traditional knowledge.

44. This is the reason why, within the Hindu civilization, rational inquiry blossomed more than empirical inquiry, as is visible in the orthodox schools of Indian philosophy.

45. Thapar, *Time as a Metaphor*, 5.

would be that even if we get it wrong in this birth, we could get it right in the next, and anyway, we have a long way to go. Thus, in the pre-modern India, says Kalpagam, "it may not be wrong to assume that measurable time had a minimal role to play in the everyday life for the majority, whose lives were regulated by the rhythms of work."[46] A cyclical sense of time finds its cultural outworking in cosmic cycles or astrology. The popular acceptance of astrology is so strong that Nirad Chaudhuri concludes that for "a Hindu, faith in his horoscope was stronger than his faith in any god or goddess or even God."[47] The practice of *Muhurtham* (a belief in auspicious/inauspicious times) by Indian Christians shows the remnant of the Hindu worldview among Indian Christians.

The indeterminate nature of cyclic time imposes another problem, which Thapar recognizes as a loss of the "differentiation between myth and history."[48] Myths, which in the Hindu tradition occupy an important role, are often relegated to an age (*yuga*) that does not correspond with human history. Myths, it is argued, "narrate events in primordial, atemporal moments which constitute sacred time and differ from the continuous profane time of daily routines."[49] Thus the distinction between myth and history is lost in the sea of endless time, where the myths are located in one of the *yugas*, which themselves are mythological.

## The Confrontation with Modern Concepts of Time

Modern British education introduced a modern understanding of time in the Indian sub-continent. In practice, this initiated dual and often parallel senses of time: the one pertaining to religio-cultural affairs retained a cyclical sense of time, while the other pertaining to the secular areas of life adopted a linear sense. The inherent ability of a Hindu to compartmentalize enables the two senses of time to operate without contradiction. As Pavan Varma discerningly remarks, the Hindu mind "is like a chest of drawers—never a single cupboard; each drawer can be a world unto itself, and can be pulled out, without reference to the others, in response to a given situation."[50]

46. Kalpagam, "Chronology and the Notion of Progress," 28.
47. Chaudhuri, *Hinduism: A Religion to Live By*, 202.
48. Thapar, *Time as a Metaphor*, 4.
49. Ibid., 25.
50. Varma, *Being Indian*, 143.

## Truth and Subjectivity, Faith and History

However, in a typical pantheistic construct that subsumes everything, it is argued that the modern linear sense of time "may be viewed as fragmentary arc(s) within the cycle," thus blurring "the dichotomy between cyclic and linear"[51] senses of time. A cycle represented by a circle that is infinitely big, with an infinite radius, would possess a circumferential arc that is a straight line, which represents linear time. The advent of a linear sense of time has nevertheless caused a rupture in the traditional way of thinking. I use the term "rupture" for two reasons: first, to represent the fragmentation of the cycle into arcs; second, to indicate that a rupture is as necessary for any socio-cultural metamorphosis as a rupturing of the pupa makes way for a beautiful butterfly. Thus when a sarcastic reference is made to *Indian Stretchable Time*, a phrase that is frequently used when someone has to wait past the designated time for others to arrive, a dichotomy is revealed between a measurable sense of time and a Hindu sense of time.

However, in recent decades, there has been an interest among some Hindu groups in founding Hindu religious beliefs on historical findings. The debate over Ayodhya as the exact birthplace of Lord Ram, or works such as *Search for the Historical Krishna*,[52] apart from their political meanderings, have questioned the traditional way in which an average Hindu is undaunted by the lack of historicity in his religious belief. This, according to Amartya Sen, is a confounding of history and religious mythology.[53] However, in light of the impending court ruling, Hindu religious leaders disingenuously have also held that Ayodhya's being the birthplace of Lord Ram is a matter of faith rather than critical enquiry.

The lack of a Hindu sense of history has also become a sensitive issue among the Hindu elite due to the superior and often contemptuous colonial attitude. Arvind Sharma writes, "The extent to which the specific charge of a lack of historical sense is a reflection of a more generally negative attitude towards Hindu civilization is difficult to pin down but should not, on that account, be completely overlooked."[54] Whatever the advantage in a linear sense of history, the feeling of superiority associated with it is an irritant.

51. Thapar, *Time as a Metaphor*, 31.

52. See Rajaram, *Search for the Historical Krishna*. Rajaram tries to unearth the history behind the myth of Krishna. He argues that Krishna, in all probability, was a historical figure who lived towards the end of the Vedic age.

53. Amartya Sen, in his inaugural address to the 61st annual session of the Indian History Congress, reiterated this in reference to Ayodhya being the birthplace of Lord Ram. Sen, "History and the Enterprise of Knowledge" in *The Hindu*, January 4, 2001, 12.

54. Sharma, *Hinduism and Its Sense of History*, 8.

## Kierkegaardian Insights for Christian Witness and Apologetics

However, as Meera Nanda claims, the Hindu apologists, particularly the Hindu right, have readily welcomed the postmodern critiques of objectivity in post-colonial writers such as Edward Said, Ashis Nandy, Claude Alvares, Gayatri Spivak, and Subaltern Studies historians. She writes, "The Hindu right combines this demand for authenticity with an essentialist understanding of culture borrowed straight from Oswald Spengler's *Decline of the West* which holds that each culture has an innate nature, a temper, which must guide all its cultural products from mathematics, to physics, to painting and poetry."[55] Accordingly, Western thinkers have no reason to feel superior about their sense of history vis-à-vis the Hindu sense of history, as that would be to use a Western standard to measure the Indian culture. This should particularly be borne in mind by Christian apologists, who assume their beliefs to be superior merely on account of them being historical and verifiable.

### Central Areas of Tensions

Although closely related, there are two separate tensions that will have to be kept distinct. The first pertains to the senses of time, where the cyclic sense of time *eliminates the incarnation of Jesus in real time history as a unique event*. The Hindu worldview contra Climacus holds that the moment of incarnation carries with it no decisiveness. The cyclic sense views history as repetitive and thus precludes the possibility of any unique occurrence in human history, such as a singular event having cosmic consequence. According to Eliade, "the cycle returns with unchanging regularity and in unchanging form . . . and all events are liable to be repeated in the next cycle."[56] A case in point is Radhakrishnan, the renowned Hindu thinker, who finds it difficult to see the incarnation of Jesus Christ as a historical event. He summarizes his idea of the incarnation of Jesus in the words of Vladimir Solovief, "This incarnation is not so much an event, which took place at one stage in history, but is something continually taking place. God is forever becoming incarnate in the world."[57] The unique historical events surrounding Christ are, from a Hindu point of view, not unique at all.

The second tension is between myth and history, where the Hindu view *tends inadvertently to mythologize the person of Jesus*. For Climacus,

---

55. Nanda, *Postmodernism and Religious Fundamentalism*, 48.
56. Thapar, *Time as a Metaphor*, 5–6.
57. Kalapati, *Dr. S. Radhakrishnan and Christianity*, 70.

such a mythologizing of the incarnation of Christ would amount to a poetizing of an otherwise humanly inconceivable story as yet another incarnation within the multitude.[58] Again, Radhakrishnan provides a case in point for the Hindu acceptance of the mythic Christ and rejection of the historic Christ. In Kalapati's words, "Radhakrishnan develops his own distinction between the *Jesus of history* and the *Christ of faith*. He commends the idea of the *Christ of faith* because it perfectly resembles his Vedantic Christ, but the historic Jesus he perceives to be a stumbling block."[59]

This cultural and theological feature of Hinduism may provide an important clue to the poor reception of Christianity in its exclusive form and an easy acceptance of Christ as one of their gods. In other words, when Christ is presented as the only and unique Savior, it is difficult for the Hindu mind to come to terms with his singularity, while having no problem in accepting Christ as one among the Hindu incarnations. The Hindu mind, which tends to relegate cultural and religious beliefs (including the Christian message) to a cyclical interpretation, would then require an accentuated historical consciousness of the Christ-event to appropriate the Christian message.

## Insights for Apologetics in the Hindu Context

The question then is, given the nature of historical consciousness in India, what is the way forward for Christian apologetics? Could it be an artificial imposition of historical rigor that is alien to the Hindu worldview, or an elimination of historical content from the Christian faith? Kierkegaard seems to recommend the Indian golden rule of a middle path. Unlike the evidential apologist, Kierkegaard finds historical inquiry an impossible vehicle to procure faith. Yet, historical content is a crucial and necessary factor for faith. Let me highlight some implications for Christians in India.

First, the historical rigor in the West, though not a result of the Christian faith, owes much to it. Christians from the very beginning, unlike Hindus, have had to refer constantly to the historical events associated with Jesus Christ as events of unparalleled significance. Historical verification came to be pivotal in the Christian message, and therefore, historical inquiry also came to have a unique place in civilizations that were predominantly Christian. The question therefore is whether we should impose such

58. PF, 35–36.
59. Kalapati, *Dr. S. Radhakrishnan and Christianity*, 70.

a rigor, which itself is a result of a long period of development in the West, as a starting point in the Indian context.

Second, although it is necessary to distinguish Christian narratives from myths, the accent would have to be on the salvific power of the biblical story. While it should be allowed that some myths are more useful than some historical events, it is necessary that one trust something real. However, we ought to recognize that the primary appeal of the Christian message is not that the biblical stories are historical but that the stories have salvific value. Belief that the biblical stories are historical is not what makes a person a Christian; rather it is the trust in the person of Jesus Christ. Further, since historical religious beliefs, like all significant historical beliefs, are frozen and transmitted through collective memory or books, they can also perhaps function as basic beliefs in Alvin Plantinga's sense of the term, rather than as beliefs that depend on some evidential support.

Third, the need for a proper appropriation of history within the community of faith is important. The practice of Eucharist in the faith community can work towards a progressive appropriation of the historical Christ-event. In other words, a believer who previously never associated history with faith can be brought into an increased awareness of historical faith through the faithful practice of Eucharist. The repeated, or shall we say, the cyclical celebration of the Lord's Table continually reminds a believer of the unique historical Christ-event until His return. The practice of Eucharist involves repetition and recollection, both of which find emphasis in Kierkegaard. As Kierkegaard's pseudonym, Constantin Constantius argues, "Repetition and recollection are the same movement, except in opposite directions, for what is recollected has been, is repeated backward, whereas genuine repetition is recollected forward."[60] Thus both recollection and repetition seek to make sense of the historical memorizing (recollecting the Cross) in the Eucharistic celebration that anticipates Christ's return (Eucharistic repetition).

Finally, a proper appropriation of history can contribute to the making of history! The supreme worth of an individual as narrated by the story of the lost sheep offers an unparalleled significance for each believer within history. That is, a person seized by what Christ has done for him has a heightened historical consciousness, and he thereby considers his role in society in obedience to the Great Commandment and the Great Commission of God, as significant. This results in social involvement leading to

---

60. *Repetition*, in FT, 131.

transformation, which is in contrast to a feeling of helplessness that is typical of the fatalistic Hindu mindset.[61] Human consciousness, which by its very nature is historical consciousness, influences the Christian faith and is likewise influenced by it.

## Conclusion

We can ask two questions: 1) Can a person accept the Christian message while remaining indifferent to its historicity? and 2) Can a person accept the Christian message without historical rigor? The answer to the first is "no!" The Christian message not only requires one to accept the historicity of the Christian message, it also requires him to understand his own existence in relation to the historical Jesus. However, the answer to the second is "yes!" A historical sense, however rudimentary, which is a necessary part of human existence, is enough for acceptance of the Christian message.

It is important to recognize that often what is considered objective historical knowledge is, in fact, a belief that is obvious only because of a spiritual revelation. Thus, Christian faith affirmation is a result of a divine encounter. Although evidential apologetics could provide an occasion for a divine encounter, the real encounter occurs at the experiential level. The value of evidential apologetics is more for someone whose spiritual eyes are already open. It is useful in helping a believer with an increased historical consciousness appreciate the truthfulness of what he believes.

It would be unproductive to reason that the empirical content of the Christian faith and its possible verification confers a superior status on Christian beliefs as opposed to Hindu beliefs. From a Kierkegaardian perspective, the leap that a historian has to take from what is historical knowledge to trust in God is not qualitatively different from the leap that a Hindu has to take from a belief in myths to a trust in the Christian message. That is, both the unbelieving historian who vouches for the historicity of Jesus events and the believer in a mythical tradition, are in the same position, if untouched by the Spirit of God who convicts the individual.

Finally, a faithful communication of the Christian message will have to take the historical nature of Christian beliefs seriously and yet acknowledge the impossibility of founding faith on historical evidence alone. Therefore,

---

61. The cyclical sense of history coupled with the idea of Karma (a belief that man's destiny is linked to his deeds in a previous birth) has led to an extremely fatalistic society that resists progress.

an apologist, apart from being conscious of the religio-cultural subtleties in a Hindu context, will have to remove obstacles within the Christian tradition that are inherited from modernistic thinking. A Kierkegaardian response may be summarized in the words of E. Stanley Jones: "a Christian witness should be just that—a witness of Jesus Christ and not his advocate."

# Bibliography

Adler, Mortimer J. *The Four Dimensions of Philosophy.* New York: Macmillan, 1993.
Agera, Cassian R. *Faith, Prayer and Grace: A Comparative Study in Rāmānuja and Kierkegaard.* Dehli: Mittal, 1987.
Allison, Henry E. "Christianity and Nonsense." In *Kierkegaard: A Collection of Critical Essays,* edited by Josiah Thompson, 289–323. New York: Anchor, 1972.
Alston, William P. "Yes, Virginia, There Is a Real World." *Proceedings and Addresses of the American Philosophical Association* 52 (1979) 779–808.
Ayer, A. J. *Language, Truth and Logic.* Middlesex, UK: Penguin, 1990.
Barrett, Lee. "The Paradox of Faith in Philosophical Fragments: Gift or Task." In *International Kierkegaard Commentary* on *Philosophical Fragments and Johannes Climacus,* vol. 7, edited by Robert L. Perkins, 261–84. Macon, GA: Mercer University Press, 1994.
Bridger, Francis. "Counseling in a Postmodern Context." In *Counseling in Context: Developing a Theological Framework,* edited by Francis Bridger et al., 275–94. London: Darton, Longman & Todd, 1998.
Bultmann, Rudolf Karl. "New Testament and Mythology." *In Kerygma and Myth, A Theological Debate,* edited by Hans Werner Bartsch, translated by R. H. Fuller, 1–44. 1941. Reprint. New York: Harper and Row, 1961.
Caputo, John D. "Instants, Secrets, and Singularities: Dealing Death in Kierkegaard and Derrida." In *Kierkegaard in Post/modernity,* edited by Martin J. Matuštík et al., 216–38. Bloomington, IN: Indiana University Press, 1995.
———. *Radical Hermeneutics: Repetition, Deconstruction, and the Hermeneutic Project.* Bloomington, IN: Indiana University Press, 1987.
Chan, Mark L. Y. *Christology from Within and Ahead: Hermeneutics, Contingency, and the Quest for Transcontextual Criteria in Christology.* Leiden: Brill, 2000.
Chaudhuri, Nirad C. *Hinduism: A Religion to Live By.* New Delhi: Oxford University Press, 1979.
Clark, Gordon H. "A Christian Appraisal of Contemporary Philosophy." *The Trinity Review* (March/April 1990) 1–6.
Clark, Kelly James. *Return to Reason.* Grand Rapids: Eerdmans, 1990.
Collingwood, R. G. *The Idea of History.* New York: Oxford University Press, 1956.
Collins, James. *The Mind of Kierkegaard.* Princeton: Princeton University Press, 1983.
Daise, Benjamin. "The Will to Truth in Kierkegaard's 'Philosophical Fragments'." *International Journal for Philosophy of Religion* 31 (1992) 1–12.
Davidson, Donald. *Inquiries into Truth and Interpretation.* Oxford: Clarendon, 1984.

## Bibliography

———. "On the Very Idea of a Conceptual Scheme." In *Inquiries into Truth and Interpretation*, 183–98. Oxford: Clarendon, 1984.

Davis, William C. "Kierkegaard on the Transformation of the Individual in Conversion." *Religious Studies* 28 (1992) 145–63.

Derrida, Jacques. *The Gift of Death*. Translated by David Wills. Chicago: University of Chicago Press, 1995.

Elrod, John. "Kierkegaard on Self and Society." In *Bibliotheca Kierkegaardiana* XI, edited by Niels Thulstrup et al., 178–96. Copenhagen: Reitzels, 1982.

Emmanuel, Steven M. *Kierkegaard and the Concept of Revelation*. Albany, NY: State University of New York, 1996.

———. "Kierkegaard on Doctrine: A Post-modern Interpretation." *Religious Studies* 25 (1989) 363–78.

Evans, C. Stephen. "Does Kierkegaard Think Beliefs can be Directly Willed?" *International Journal for Philosophy of Religion* 26 (1989) 173–84.

———. "Empiricism, Rationalism, and the Possibility of Historical Religious Knowledge." In *Christian Perspectives on Religious Knowledge*, edited by C. Stephen Evans et al., 134–60. Grand Rapids: Eerdmans, 1993.

———. *Faith Beyond Reason: A Kierkegaardian Account*. Grand Rapids: Eerdmans, 1998.

———. "Is Kierkegaard an Irrationalist? Reason, Paradox and Faith." *Religious Studies* 25 (1989) 347–62.

———. "Kierkegaard's View of the Unconscious." In *Kierkegaard in Post/modernity*, edited by Martin J. Matuštík et al., 76–97. Bloomington, IN: Indiana University Press, 1995.

———. *Passionate Reason*. Bloomington, IN: Indiana University Press, 1992.

———. "Realism and Antirealism in Kierkegaard's Concluding Unscientific Postscript." In *The Cambridge Companion to Kierkegaard*, edited by Alastair Hannay et al., 154–76. Cambridge: Cambridge University Press, 1998.

———. "The Relevance of Historical Evidence for Christian Faith: A Critique of a Kierkegaardian View." *Faith and Philosophy* 7 (1990) 470–85.

Ferreira, M. Jamie. "Faith and the Kierkegaardian Leap." In *The Cambridge Companion to Kierkegaard*, edited by Alastair Hannay et al., 207–34. Cambridge: Cambridge University Press, 1998.

———. "'The Next Thing': On the Maieutic Relations between the 'Upbuilding Discourses in Various Spirits' and 'Works of Love.'" In *International Kierkegaard Commentary vol. 15 on Upbuilding Discourses in Various Spirits*, edited by Robert L. Perkins, 371–96. Macon GA: Mercer University Press, 2005.

Flew, Anthony. "Miracles." In *The Encyclopedia of Philosophy*, edited by Paul Edwards, 5:346–53. New York: Macmillan and The Free Press, 1967.

Fraser, Nancy. "Foucault on Modern Power: Empirical Insights and Normative Confusions." In *Unruly Practices: Power, Discourse and Gender in Contemporary Social Theory*, edited by Nancy Fraser, 17–34. Minneapolis: University of Minnesota Press, 1989.

Frederick, Sontag. "Is God Really in History?" *Religious Studies* 15 (1979) 379–90.

Friedman, R. Z. "Kant and Kierkegaard: The Limits of Reason and the Cunning of Faith." *International Journal for Philosophy of Religion* 19 (1986) 3–22.

———. "Kierkegaard: First Existentialist or Last Kantian?" *Religious Studies* 18 (1982) 159–70.

Fuller, B. A. G. *A History of Philosophy*. 3rd ed. New York: Rinehart and Winston, 1938.

Gardiner, Patrick. *Kierkegaard*. Oxford: Oxford University Press, 1988.

## Bibliography

Garelick, Herbert M. *The Anti-Christianity of Kierkegaard: A Study of Concluding Unscientific Postscript*. The Hague: Nijhoff, 1965.
Geisler, Norman L. *Christian Apologetics*. Grand Rapids: Baker, 1976.
———. *Miracles and Modern Thought*. Grand Rapids: Zondervan, 1982.
Gellner, Ernest. *Postmodernism, Reason and Religion*. London: Routledge, 1992.
———. "Relativism and Universals." In *Rationality and Relativism*, edited by Martin Hollis et al., 181–200. Cambridge: MIT, 1982.
Gouwens, David J. "Kierkegaard on the Universally Religious and the Specifically Christian." In *Kierkegaard and Religious Pluralism*, edited by Andrew J. Burgess, 83–104. Eugene, OR: Wipf and Stock, 2007.
———. "Kierkegaard's Understanding of Doctrine." *Modern Theology* 5 (1988) 13–22.
Grenz, Stanley J. *A Primer on Postmodernism*. Grand Rapids: Eerdmans, 1996.
Grenz, Stanley J., and Roger E. Olson. *20th Century Theology*. Downers Grove, IL: InterVarsity, 1992.
Harrison, Victoria S. "Kierkegaard's Philosophical Fragments: A Clarification." *Religious Studies* 33 (1997) 455–63.
Harvey, Van A. *The Historian and the Believer*. New York: Macmillan, 1966.
Hegel, G. W. F. *The Phenomenology of Mind*. Translated by J. B. Baillie. New York: Macmillan, 1931.
Henriksen, Jan-Olav. *The Reconstruction of Religion: Lessing, Kierkegaard and Nietzsche*. Grand Rapids: Eerdmans, 2001.
Heywood Thomas, John. *Subjectivity and Paradox*. Oxford: Blackwell, 1957.
Hicks, Peter. *Evangelicals and Truth: A Creative Proposal for a Postmodern Age*. Leicester, UK: Apollos, 1998.
Hogg, Alfred G. *Karma and Redemption*. Madras: Christian Literature Society, 1909.
Hughes, Edward J. "How Subjectivity is Truth in the 'Concluding Unscientific Postscript.'" *Religious Studies* 31 (1995) 197–208.
Hume, David. *Dialogues concerning Natural Religion*. Edited by Henry D. Aiken. New York: Hafner, 1948.
———. *An Inquiry Concerning Human Understanding*. Edited by C. W. Hendel. New York: Bobbs-Merrill, 1955.
Hustwit, Ronald. "Adler and the Ethical: A Study of Kierkegaard's 'On Authority and Revelation.'" *Religious Studies* 21 (1985) 331–48.
Ingraffia, Brian D. *Postmodern Theory and Biblical Theology: Vanquishing God's Shadow*. Cambridge: Cambridge University Press, 1995.
Jahan, Ishrat. "The Social Construction of 'Self' and Womanhood in a Hindu Village of Bangladesh." *Journal of World Anthropology: Occassional Papers*, 3 (2007) 41–51.
John, Varughese. "Being in the Truth: Climacus' Devout Idolater from within Rāmānuja's Viśiṣṭādvaitic Tradition." *ACTA KIERKEGAARDIANA–Kierkegaard: East and West* 5 (2011) 78–88.
Kalapati, Joshua. *Dr. S. Radhakrishnan and Christianity: An Introduction to Hindu-Christian Apologetics*. New Delhi: ISPCK, 2002.
Kalpagam, U. "Chronology and the Notion of Progress." *Journal of Indian Council of Philosophical Research*–Special Issue (June 2001) 25–42.
Kant, Immanuel. *Critique of Pure Reason*. Translated by Norman Kemp Smith. New York: St. Martin's, 1965.
Kivela, Jyrki. "Kierkegaard on Miracles: Introductory Observations." *Søren Kierkegaard Newsletter* 43 (2002) 11–15.

# Bibliography

Kärkkäinen, Veli-Matti. *Pneumatology: The Holy Spirit in Ecumenical, International, and Contextual Perspective.* Grand Rapids: Baker Academic, 2002.

Leibniz, Gottfried Wilhelm. *Monadology and other Philosophical Writings.* Translated by Robert Latta. London: Oxford University Press, 1898.

Lessing, Gotthold. "On the Proof of the Spirit and of Power." In *Lessing's Theological Writings*, edited and translated by Henry Chadwick. Stanford: Stanford University, 1957.

Lewis, C. S. *Miracles.* New York: Macmillan, 1969.

———. *Chronicles of Narnia: The Horse and His Boy.* New York: HarperCollins, 1994.

Lewis, Charles. "Kierkegaard, Nietzsche and the Faith of our Fathers." *International Journal for Philosophy of Religion* 20 (1986) 3–16.

Lindbeck, George. *The Nature of Doctrine: Religion and Theology in a Postliberal Age.* Philadelphia: Westminster, 1984.

Lipner, Julius. *The Face of Truth: A Study of the Meaning and Metaphysics in the Vedāntic Theology of Rāmānuja.* Albany, NY: State University of New York, 1986.

Lippitt, John. "A Funny Thing Happened to me on the Way to Salvation: Climacus as Humorist in Kierkegaard's 'Concluding Unscientific Postscript.'" *Religious Studies* 33 (1997) 181–202.

Loewenberg, J. *Hegel Selections.* New York: Scribner's Sons, 1929.

Lowrie, Walter. *Kierkegaard.* Oxford: Oxford University Press, 1938.

Lyotard, Francois Jean. *The Postmodern Condition: A Report on Knowledge.* Manchester, UK: Manchester University Press, 1986.

Mackey, Louis. "The Poetry of Inwardness." In *Kierkegaard: A Collection of Critical Essays*, edited by Josiah Thompson, 1–102. New York: Doubleday, 1972.

Malantschuk, Gregor. *Kierkegaard's Way to the Truth: An Introduction to the Authorship of Søren Kierkegaard.* Montreal: Inter Editions, 1987.

Marino, Gordon D. "Is Madness Truth, Is Fanaticism Faith?" *International Journal for Philosophy of Religion* 22 (1987) 41–53.

Matuštík, Martin J., and Merold Westphal. *Kierkegaard in Post/modernity.* Bloomington, IN: Indiana University Press, 1995.

McIntyre, John. *The Shape of Pneumatology: Studies in the Doctrine of the Holy Spirit.* Edinburgh: T. & T. Clark, 1997.

Mehl, Peter J. "Despair's Demand: An Appraisal of Kierkegaard's Argument for God." *International Journal for Philosophy of Religion* 32 (1992) 167–82.

Mitchell, Basil. "Faith and Reason: A False Antithesis?" *Religious Studies* 16 (1980) 131–44.

Mooney, Edward F. "Abraham and Dilemma: Kierkegaard's Theological Suspension Revisited." *International Journal for Philosophy of Religion* 19 (1986) 23–41.

Moser, Paul K. *Philosophy after Objectivity: Making Sense in Perspective.* Oxford: Oxford University Press, 1993.

Muller, Paul. *Meddelelsensdialektik i Søren Kierkegaards Philosophiske Smuler.* Copenhagen: C.A. Reitzels, 1979.

Murphy, John P. *Pragmatism: From Peirce to Davidson.* Boulder, CO: Westview, 1990.

Nanda, Meera. *Postmodernism and Religious Fundamentalism: A Scientific Rebuttal to Hindu Science.* Pondicherry, India: Navayana, 2003.

Newton-Smith, W. "Relativism and the Possibility of Interpretation." In *Rationality and Relativism*, edited by Martin Hollis et al., 106–22. 1982. Reprint. Cambridge: MIT, 1984.

# Bibliography

Nietzsche, Friedrich. "On Truth and Lie in an Extra-Moral Sense." In *The Portable Nietzsche*, edited by Walter Kaufmann, 42-50. New York: Viking, 1968.
Olson, Roger E. *The Story of Christian Theology: Twenty Centuries of Tradition and Reform*. Secunderabad, India: O.M., 1999.
Perkins, Robert L. *International Kierkegaard Commentary: The Sickness unto Death*. Macon, GA: Mercer University Press, 1987.
Phillips, D. Z. *The Concept of Prayer*. London: Routledge and Kegan Paul, 1965.
Plantinga, Alvin. *God and Other Minds*. Ithaca, NY: Cornell University Press, 1967.
———. "Reason and Belief in God." In *Faith and Rationality*, edited by Alvin Plantinga et al., 16-93. South Bend, IN: University of Notre Dame Press, 1983.
Plato. *Meno*. Translated by W. R. M. Lamb. Cambridge: Harvard University Press, 1924.
Pojman, Louis. "Kierkegaard on Faith and Freedom." *International Journal for Philosophy of Religion* 27 (1990) 41-61.
———. "Kierkegaard on Faith and History." *International Journal for Philosophy of Religion* 13 (1982) 57-68.
———. "Kierkegaard on Freedom and the Scala Paradisi." *International Journal for Philosophy of Religion* 18 (1985) 141-48.
———. *The Logic of Subjectivity: Kierkegaard's Philosophy of Religion*. Tuscaloosa, AL: University of Alabama Press, 1984.
Poole, Roger. *Kierkegaard: The Indirect Communication*. Charlottesville, VA: The University Press of Virginia, 1993.
———. "The Unknown Kierkegaard: Twentieth-Century Receptions." In *The Cambridge Companion to Kierkegaard*, edited by Alastair Hannay et al., 48-75. Cambridge: Cambridge University Press, 1998.
Pradhan, R. C. "On the Very Idea of Relative Truth." *Journal of Indian Council of Philosophical Research* 17 (2000) 43-62.
Putnam, Hillary. *Realism with a Human Face*. Edited by James Conant. Cambridge: Harvard University Press, 1990.
———. "Realism and Reason." *Proceedings and Addresses of the American Philosophical Association* 50 (1977) 483-97.
———. *Reason, Truth and History*. Cambridge: Cambridge University Press, 1981.
Rabinow, Paul. *The Foucault Reader*. New York: Pantheon, 1984.
Rae, Murray A. "The Forgetfulness of Historical-Talkative Remembrance in Kierkegaard's Practice in Christianity." In *International Kierkegaard Commentary* on *Practice in Christianity*, vol. 20, edited by Robert L. Perkins, 69-94. Macon GA: Mercer University Press, 2004.
———. "Kierkegaard and the Historians." *International Journal for Philosophy of Religion* 37 (1995) 87-102.
———. *Kierkegaard's Vision of the Incarnation: A Faith Transformed*. Oxford: Clarendon, 1997.
Raghavachar, S. S. "The Spiritual Vision of Rāmānuja." In *Hindu Spirituality: Vedas through Vedanta*, edited by Krishna Sivaraman, 261-74. New York: Crossroad, 1989.
Rajaram N. S. *Search for the Historical Krishna*. Bangalore: Prism, 2004.
Ramm, Bernard. *After Fundamentalism: The Future of Evangelical Theology*. San Francisco: Harper & Row, 1983.
Raschke, Carl. *The Next Reformation: Why Evangelicals Must Embrace Postmodernity*. Grand Rapids: Baker Academic, 2004.

## Bibliography

Redmond, Walter. "A Logic of Faith." *International Journal for Philosophy of Religion* 27 (1990) 165–80.

Ricoeur, Paul. "Philosophy after Kierkegaard." In *Kierkegaard: A Critical Reader*, edited by Jonathan Ree et al., 9–25. Oxford: Blackwell, 1998.

Rogers, Jack B. and Baird E. Forrest, *Introduction to Philosophy: A Case Method Approach*. San Francisco: Harper and Row, 1981.

Rorty, Richard. *Objectivity, Relativism and Truth: Philosophical Papers*. Cambridge: Cambridge University Press, 1991.

Sagi, Avi. "The Suspension of the Ethical and the Religious Meaning of Ethics in Kierkegaard's Thought." *International Journal for Philosophy of Religion* 32 (1992) 83–103.

Sands, Paul Francis. *The Justification of Religious Faith in Søren Kierkegaard, John Henry Newman, and William James*. Piscataway, NJ: Gorgias, 2004.

Schleiermacher, Friedrich. *The Christian Faith*. 2 vols. Translated and edited by H. R. MacKintosh et al., New York: Harper and Row, 1963.

Schrag, Calvin O. "The Kierkegaard-Effect in the Shaping of the Contours of Modernity." In *Kierkegaard in Post/modernity*, edited by Martin J. Matuštík et al., 1–17. Bloomington, IN: Indiana University Press, 1995.

Sen, Amartya. "History and the Enterprise of Knowledge." *The Hindu*, January 4. 2001, 12.

Sharma, Arvind. *Hinduism and Its Sense of History*. New Delhi: Oxford University Press, 2003.

Solomon, Robert C. *From Rationalism to Existentialism: The Existentialists and their Nineteenth-Century Backgrounds*. 1972. Reprint. Lanham, MD: Rowman & Littlefield, 2001.

———. "The Secret of Hegel (Kierkegaard's Complaint): A Study in Hegel's Philosophy of Religion." *Philosophical Forum* 9 (1977–78) 440–58.

Spier, J. M. *Christianity and Existentialism*. Philadelphia: Presbyterian and Reformed, 1953.

Spinoza, Baruch. *Tractatus theologico-politicus*. Translated by Samuel Shirley. Leiden: Brill, 1991.

Steffes, Harald. "Kierkegaard's Germanophone Socrates Sources." In *Kierkegaard and the Greek World*, Tome I: *Socrates and Plato*, edited by Jon Stewart et al., 267–311. Kierkegaard Research: Sources, Reception, and Resources series, 2. Farnham, UK: Ashgate, 2010.

Stirling, Hutchinson James. *The Secret of Hegel*. London: Longmans, Roberts, and Green, 1865.

Stott, Michelle. *Behind the Mask: Kierkegaard's Pseudonymic Treatment of Lessing in the Concluding Unscientific Postscript*. Lewisburg, PA: Bucknell University Press, 1993.

Stumpf, Enoch Samuel. *Socrates to Sartre: A History of Philosophy*. Delhi: McGraw Hill, 1966.

Taylor, Charles. *Hegel*. Cambridge: Cambridge University Press, 1975.

———. *Sources of the Self*. Cambridge: Harvard University Press, 1989.

Taylor, Mark C. *Kierkegaard's Pseudonymous Authorship: A Study of Time and the Self*. Princeton: Princeton University Press, 1975.

Thapar, Romila. "Time as a Metaphor of History." In *History and Beyond*. New Delhi: Oxford University Press, 1996.

Thilly, Frank. *A History of Philosophy*. NY: Henry Holt & Company, 1940.

# Bibliography

Thorslev, Peter. "German Romantic Idealism." In *Cambridge Companion to British Romanticism*, edited by Stuart Curran, 82–102. Cambridge: Cambridge University Press, 2010.

Tillich, Paul. *The Dynamics of Faith*. New York: Harper & Row, 1957.

Tosh, John. *The Pursuit of History: Aims, Methods and New Directions in the Study of Modern History*. 3rd ed. Harlow, UK: Longman, 1999.

Varma, Pavan K. *Being Indian*. New Delhi: Viking, 2004.

*The Vedānta-Sūtras with the Commentary of Rāmānuja*. Translated by George Thibaut. Delhi: Motilal, 1904.

Walsh, Sylvia. "On 'Feminine' and 'Masculine' Forms of Despair." In *International Kierkegaard Commentary: The Sickness Unto Death*, edited by Robert L. Perkins, 121–34. Macon: Mercer University Press, 1987.

———. "Kierkegaard and Postmodernism." *International Journal for Philosophy of Religion* 29 (1991) 113–22.

Ward, Keith. "Miracles and Testimony." *Religious Studies* 21 (1985) 131–45.

Watkin, Julia. *Kierkegaard*. London: Chapman, 1997.

Westphal, Merold. "Climacus on Subjectivity and the System." *Kierkegaard's Concluding Unscientific Postscript: A Critical Guide*, edited by Rick Anthony Furtak, 132–48. Cambridge: Cambridge University Press, 2010.

———. "Kierkegaard and Hegel." In *The Cambridge Companion to Kierkegaard*, edited by Alastair Hannay et al., 101–24. Cambridge: Cambridge University Press, 1998.

———. "Kierkegaard and the Logic of Insanity." *Religious Studies* 7 (1971) 193–211.

———. "Kierkegaard's Psychology and Unconscious Despair." In *International Kierkegaard Commentary: The Sickness unto Death*, edited by Robert L. Perkins, 39–66. Macon, GA: Mercer University Press, 1987.

———. *Overcoming Onto-theology: Toward a Postmodern Christian Faith*. New York: Fordham University Press, 2001.

Whittaker, John H. "Kierkegaard on History and Faith." *Scottish Journal of Theology* 40 (1987) 379–97.

Williams, Clifford. "Kierkegaardian Suspicion and Properly Basic Beliefs." *Religious Studies* 30 (1994) 261–67.

Williams, Rheinallt Nantlais. *Faith Facts History Science: and How They Fit Together*. Chicago: Tyndale, 1973.

Wisdo, David M. "Kierkegaard on Belief, Faith and Explanation." *International Journal for Philosophy of Religion* 21 (1987) 95–114.

———. "Kierkegaard on the Limits of Christian Epistemology." *International Journal for Philosophy of Religion* 29 (1991) 97–112.

Wittgenstein, Ludwig. *Culture and Value*. Translated by Peter Winch. Chicago: University of Chicago Press, 1980.

Zizioulas, John D. *Being as Communion: Studies in Personhood and the Church*. Crestwood, NY: Vladimir's Seminary Press, 1985.

# Index

Abraham, 32, 36, 53–55, 60
Absolute, 7, 9, 15–16, 18–19
   certitude, 109
   good, 20
   monism, 62
   other, 36, 50, 53–56
   paradox, 84, 95, 118, 134
   relation, 41
   teacher, 39, 47, 65, 105, 115, 118
absolutism, 10, 19
Adam/Adamic, 27, 43, 48
aesthetic(s), 15, 33, 47
agency/agencies, 22
analytical, 14, 46
anthropology/anthropological, 17, 20, 35–36, 41
Anti-Climacus, 26, 30, 36, 38, 42–43, 49, 51, 74, 94
anti-realism, 3, 18, 78
apologist/apologetics, 46, 82, 98–99, 115, 123–31, 135, 137, 141–42, 144–45
apostle(s), 55, 86–87, 130, 135
approximat(ive)(ely)/approximating/approximation(s), 41, 52, 58–59, 61, 78, 88, 107–8, 110–11
Aristotle, 3, 45
Augustine/Augustinian/Augustinianism, 17, 23–25, 27, 37, 134
Ayodhya, 73, 140

baptism, 27
Barrett, Lee, 25, 64
Bible/biblical, 29, 61, 83, 87, 127

Bultmann, Rudolf, 46, 83, 86, 94

Calvin/Calvinistic, 23
Caputo, John, 17, 53–55
certitude, 39, 47, 81, 105, 107–9, 117, 130
Chardin, Teilhard de, 46
Chaudhuri, Nirad, 139
Christendom, 17, 28, 32, 124–25, 137
Christology/christological, 83, 133, 135–36
chronotic, 101
civilization(s), 137–38, 140, 142
cognitive, 4, 27, 29, 33, 36, 38, 43, 46, 93, 105, 130
Collingwood, R G, 75–77, 79–80
communal, xvii, 14, 51
Comte, Auguste, 74
conceptual/conceptualism, 3, 8–11, 31, 46, 64, 77
consciousness, 16, 21, 25–26, 36, 81, 84, 88, 98, 104, 106, 134, 142–44
Constantine, 6
Constantius, Constantine, 143
contemporaneity/contemporaneous, xviii, 23, 116, 118–21
contingent/contingency, 17, 19–21, 48, 80–81, 83, 86, 106–7, 117
contradiction, 10–12, 18, 28–30, 41, 51, 105, 107, 139
correspondence, 3–4, 14–15, 129, 138

deception, 37–38, 45, 125
deconstruction, 14, 54
demythologize/demythologizing, 82

155

# Index

Denmark, ix–x, 35, 61, 70
Derrida, Jacques, 14, 36, 53–55
Descartes, René/Cartesian, ix–xi, 4, 17, 34, 50
dialectic/dialectical, 23, 33, 36, 38, 83, 87, 98, 101–103, 106, 108, 126
Dilthey, Wilhelm, 77
dogma(s)/dogmatic/dogmatism, xi, 8, 69

earnest(ly)/earnestness, 28, 41, 52, 118
election, 23
Eliade, Mircea, 138, 141
Elrod, John, 53
emancipate/emancipation, 5, 7, 51
Emmanuel, Steven, 28, 31, 101, 113
empiricist/empiricism, xviii, 5, 89–91, 93–94, 97, 118
epistemic/epistemology/epistemological, xviii, 19, 53, 82–83, 86, 107, 117, 122, 131–32
eternal consciousness (see consciousness)
ethics/ethical, 5, 33, 36, 38, 43–44, 47–50, 54–55, 62, 79–80, 99
ethnocentric, xiv, 8–11, 32
Eucharist, 143
evangelical, 127, 130
Evans, Stephen C, 49–50, 53, 76, 78–79, 84–85, 93–94, 105, 108, 113–17, 122, 131–32
evidential/evidentialism, 13–14, 82, 98–99, 117, 124, 126–28, 130–31, 142–44
existential, ix, 5, 15, 35, 41, 43, 83, 98, 101

falsification, 88, 111, 114
fatalistic/fatalism, 23–24, 144
Ferreira, Jamie, 46, 70
Fichte, Johann Gottlieb, 15
finitude, 17–20, 48
Flew, Antony, 89, 92–93
Foucault Michel/ Foucaultian, 6–7, 9, 14, 20, 77

Gellner, Ernest, 10

Harvey, Van, 94
Hegel/Hegelian, 7, 15–17, 20, 35, 44–46, 51, 53, 68, 116, 125, 133–34
hermeneutic(s), 17, 19–20, 48, 77
Hick, John, 74, 86
Hindu, xiv, 62, 64, 74, 137–42, 144–45
historiography, 75, 85
historical consciousness (see consciousness)
Hogg, A G, 137
Hume, David/Humean, 89–92, 97, 109, 127–28

idealism, 3, 15, 77
identity, 5, 20, 50, 100
ideology, 7
idolater (penitent/devout), xiv, xviii, 17, 27, 41, 58–63, 65, 67–70
*imago dei*, 51
imitation/*imitatio Christi*, 33, 51, 55, 118, 123, 126, 135
immanence, 88, 100–101, 115
indirect (communication/method), 124–25
individualism, 50–51
instrumentalist/instrumentalized, 6, 103
inward/inwardness, 15, 20–21, 35, 39–42, 46, 100–102
irony, xi, 20, 112
irrationalist/irrationalism/irrationality, xi, 52, 108
Isaac, 32, 53–55, 60, 96

Jesus of history (historical Jesus), xviii, 83, 86, 98, 102, 113, 121, 137, 142, 144
*jñānā*, 62–63
Jones, Stanley E, 145
Judas, 124
justification, 8, 11, 31, 41, 109–10, 124, 126

## Index

*kairotic*, 101
Kant, Immanuel/Kantian, 15–16, 18, 77–78
*karma*, 62–63, 137, 144

law (moral/Mosaic), 28, 55, 61, 101, 123
leap (of faith), 45–47, 95, 110, 117–18, 121, 126, 144
Leibniz, Gottfried, 85–86
Lessing, Gotthold, xviii, 19, 45, 49, 61, 68–69, 78, 85, 99, 106–7, 116–19, 121, 125
Levinas, Emmanuel, 55
Lewis C S, 20, 70, 91
liberal/liberalism, 16, 74, 82, 84, 98
Lindbeck, George, 31
linguistic, 17, 31–32
Lyotard, Jean-François, 7, 20

*mārga*, 62
Marx/Marxian, 7, 51
McIntyre, John, 134
*Meno*, 21, 64
metanarrative(s), 7, 20, 138
metaphor(s), 6, 138–41
metaphysics, 3, 13, 16
midwife/midwifery, 21, 28, 129
mimesis/mimetic, 17, 55, 57
miracle(s)/miraculous, xviii, 23, 83–85, 87, 89–98, 103, 116–17, 119, 121–22, 130, 133, 136
missionary/missionaries, 125, 137
moment, 8, 12, 21, 26, 101, 118–119, 126, 137
  of faith, 27–28, 37, 66, 97, 99, 102, 133
  of incarnation, 27, 33, 58, 99–102, 126, 128, 133, 137, 141
  of truth, 21
moral/morality, 6, 9, 15, 21, 32, 35, 44, 54–55, 74, 95
Moser, Paul K, 11, 76–77
Mynster, Bishop, 69
myth(s)/mythical/mythology/mythological, 73–74, 83, 85–86, 98, 100, 107, 138–44

Nandy, Ashis, 141
Narnia, 70
narrative, 7, 20, 55, 73, 86, 138, 143
naturalistic, 5, 81–82, 85, 93
neighbor, 55–57
Nietzsche, Friedrich, 6–7, 32, 41
nihilism, 6, 35
noumenal, 18

offence, 84, 102, 105, 126, 129, 132
ontological/ontologically, 37, 43, 47, 50, 53, 57, 77, 135
ontotheology, 18, 84
orthodox/orthodoxy, 16, 30, 81, 102, 131, 136, 138

pagan(s)/paganism, 17, 21, 26, 29, 60, 107, 125
Paley, William, 127
pantheist/pantheistic/pantheism, 16, 133, 140
paradox/paradoxical, 25–26, 40, 46, 53, 84, 86, 95, 101, 107–8, 115, 118–19, 129, 133–34
Paul/Pauline, 17, 26, 36–37, 123, 129–130, 135
Pelagius/Pelagianism, 23, 25
phenomena/phenomenal, 18, 129
Phillips, D. Z., 53
Pilate, Pontius, 3, 42–43
Plantinga, Alvin, 13, 131–32, 143
Plato/Platonic/Platonism, 12, 21, 64, 85–86, 93
pluralistic/pluralism, 62, 65
Pneumatology/pneumatalogical, xviii, 37, 133–36
poetry/poetic/poetizing, 22, 141–42
Pojman, Louis, 22–23, 39–40, 43, 100
positivist(s)/positivistic/positivism, xviii, 5, 13, 74–76, 81–82, 98
postmodern/postmodernity/postmodernism, xi, xiv, xvii, 4–9, 12, 17–20, 31, 33, 35, 54, 82–83, 141
pragmatic/pragmatist(s)/pragmatism, 4, 8–9
*prapatti*, 63, 65, 68

*Index*

pre-theoretical, 12–13, 19, 92, 97, 126
prodigal, 29
prototype/prototypal, 51, 55–57, 111–12, 135
pseudonym/pseudonymous, x, 25–26, 38, 59–60, 85, 99, 101, 116, 143
Putnam, Hilary, 10–11, 76

qualitative/qualitatively, 11, 19, 46, 66, 108, 121, 144

Radhakrishnan, Sarvepalli, 141–42
Rāmānuja, xiv, 62, 67–70
rationalist/rationalism, xi, xviii, 5, 12, 34–35, 46, 81, 85, 90–91, 93–94, 108, 116–18, 124–25, 130
realist/realism, 3, 8–11, 14, 76–78, 105
recollect/recollecting/recollection, 24, 28, 64, 99, 143
reformation, 129–30
relative, 8, 10–12, 43, 54
repetition, 48, 57, 138, 143
representational, 3, 15
resurrection, 84–85, 109, 121
revelation, xviii, 14, 25–26, 28, 32, 61, 65, 87, 95, 101, 113, 125, 127–28, 135, 144
Rorty, Richard, xiv, xvii, 8–9, 11

Said, Edward, 141
salvation, 22, 25, 28, 37, 62–63, 84–85, 101, 137
scandal/scandalized, 29, 129
Schelling, Friedrich Wilhelm Joseph, 15
scheme, xiv, 8–11, 19, 32–33, 50, 93, 100
Schleiermacher, Friedrich, 30–31
Schrag, Calvin O, 32–33, 100–101
Scripture(s), 28, 81–83, 86–89, 112, 117, 134
self-deception (see deception)
semantic, xvii, 12, 31, 43, 130
Sen, Amartya, xi, 73, 140

Sharma, Arvind, 140
Silentio, Johannes de, x, 32, 45
sin, 16–18, 22–23, 25–28, 36–37, 62, 70, 126, 128, 144
sin-consciousness (see consciousness)
socialist/socialistic, 5
sociocultural, 8, 31, 32, 140
Socrates, xvii, 14, 21–22, 39, 62, 64, 68–69, 99–100, 102, 125
Socratic Method, 64, 128, 136
solidarity, xvii, 8–9, 14, 21
Solovief, Vladimir, 141
speculative/speculatively, 7, 15–17, 20, 35, 40, 60, 79, 138
Spengler, Oswald, 141
Spinoza, Baruch, 85–86, 95
Spirit/spirit (xiii, xv, 31–32, 37, 44, 60, 69, 81, 86–87, 94, 97, 112, 116, 129–30, 133–36, 144
Spivak, Gayatri, 141
*sub specie aeterni*, 5, 40
subjective/subjectivity, xi, xvii, xviii, 14–15, 19, 23–24, 31, 34, 39–45, 47–50, 52, 58, 60–62, 65–68, 78–79, 102, 104, 114–15, 130–31
subjectivism, 39, 58, 100
supralapsarianism, 23
suspicion(s), xvii, 6, 17, 19–20, 23, 77–78, 109

Taylor, Charles, 34, 36
Taylor, Mark C, 24–25, 99, 101
teacher, 21–22, 24–26, 30, 33, 39, 43, 47, 64–66, 68, 74, 99–100, 105, 115, 118, 120, 132
teleological, 45, 55, 127
temporal, 12, 88, 94, 99, 101, 112, 139
Thapar, Romila, 138–41
theology/theological, 5, 18, 30, 35, 37, 53, 68, 74, 77, 83–84, 94, 111, 116–18, 129, 134, 142
theory/theories, 3–5, 8, 18, 31, 41, 47, 64, 82, 112, 129
Tillich, Paul, 83–84, 108
trans-cultural, 8–9
transition, 32, 45–47, 105, 117, 121

Trinity/trinitarian, 121, 133–36
Troeltsch, Ernst/Troeltschian, 82–83, 86

"ugly broad ditch", xviii, 61, 99, 106, 116, 118, 121

Varma, Pavan, 139
*Vedānta*, 62
verification (empirical/historical), 81, 90, 137–38, 142, 144
vocabulary, 9
volition/volitional, 23–24, 26, 36–38

Westphal, Merold, 7, 15–16, 18, 20, 39, 50–51, 60
will (act of)/willing/willful, x, 23–28, 34, 36–40, 44, 52, 57, 62–63, 68, 103–4, 116
witness/witnessed/eyewitness, 6, 34, 73, 87–88, 92, 105, 109–12, 119, 121, 123, 133, 145
worldview(s), 18, 83, 139, 141–42

zeitgeist, 82, 84
Zizioulas, John, 135–36

www.ingramcontent.com/pod-product-compliance
Lightning Source LLC
Chambersburg PA
CBHW050816160426
43192CB00010B/1778